SEASONS
OF
LEXINGTON

The Greater Lexington Chamber of Commerce and Community Communications, Inc., would like to express our gratitude to the following companies for their leadership in the development of this book.

Library of Congress Cataloging-in-Publication Data

Clark, Thomas Dionysius, 1903-
    Seasons of Lexington/special introductory by Thomas Clark;
    editorial essays by Thomas Clark; photography by Jeff Rogers and
    Pat McDonogh; profiles written by Pam Mitchell Mangas; profile
    photography by Stewart Bowman and David Coyle.—1st ed.
    p. cm.
  Includes bibliographical references and index.
  ISBN 1-58192-027-X
  1. Lexington (Ky.)—Civilization. 2. Lexington (Ky.)—Pictorial works.
3. Seasons—Kentucky—Lexington. 4. Seasons—Kentucky—Lexington—
Pictorial works. 5. Lexington (Ky.)—Economic conditions. 6. Business
enterprises—Kentucky—Lexington.   I. Mangas, Pam Mitchell, 1971-
II. Title.
F459.L6 C58 2001
976.9'47—dc21   2001002587

SEASONS
OF
LEXINGTON

SPECIAL INTRODUCTION BY *Dr. Thomas Clark*
FEATURING THE PHOTOGRAPHY OF *Jeff Rogers and Pat McDonogh*
CORPORATE PROFILES BY *Pam Mitchell Mangas*
CORPORATE PROFILE PHOTOGRAPHY BY *Stewart Bowman and David Coyle*

SEASONS
OF
LEXINGTON

SPECIAL INTRODUCTION BY *Dr. Thomas Clark*
EDITORIAL ESSAYS BY *Dr. Thomas Clark*
FEATURING THE PHOTOGRAPHY OF *Jeff Rogers and Pat McDonogh*
CORPORATE PROFILES BY *Pam Mitchell Mangas*
CORPORATE PROFILE PHOTOGRAPHY BY *Stewart Bowman and David Coyle*

COMMUNITY COMMUNICATIONS, INC.
PUBLISHER: *Ronald P. Beers*

STAFF FOR *SEASONS OF LEXINGTON*
ACQUISITIONS: *Ronald P. Beers*
PUBLISHER'S SALES ASSOCIATE: *Marie Perdue*
EDITOR IN CHIEF: *Wendi L. Lewis*
MANAGING EDITOR: *Angela C. Johnson*
PROFILE EDITOR: *Mary Catherine Richardson*
DESIGN DIRECTOR: *Scott Phillips*
DESIGNER: *Ramona Davis*
PHOTO EDITORS: *Angela C. Johnson and Ramona Davis*
CONTRACT MANAGER: *Christi Stevens*
NATIONAL SALES MANAGER: *Ronald P. Beers*
SALES ASSISTANT: *Sandra Akers*
EDITORIAL ASSISTANTS: *Krewe Maynard and Eleanor Planer*
ACQUISITIONS COORDINATOR: *Angela P. White*
ACCOUNTING SERVICES: *Stephanie Perez*
PRINT PRODUCTION MANAGER: *Jarrod Stiff*
PRE-PRESS AND SEPARATIONS: *Artcraft Graphic Productions*

CCI

COMMUNITY COMMUNICATIONS, INC.
MONTGOMERY, ALABAMA

David M. Williamson, CHIEF EXECUTIVE OFFICER
Ronald P. Beers, PRESIDENT
W. David Brown, CHIEF OPERATING OFFICER

© 2001 COMMUNITY COMMUNICATIONS
ALL RIGHTS RESERVED
PUBLISHED 2001
PRINTED IN USA
FIRST EDITION
LIBRARY OF CONGRESS CATALOG NUMBER: 2001002587
ISBN NUMBER: 1-58192-027-X

*Every effort has been made to ensure the accuracy of the information herein.
However, the authors and Community Communications are not responsible
for any errors or omissions that might have occurred.*

Part One

Spring 16

When the last basketball has been dribbled, and the Keeneland Race Course has become host to a new crop of Derby hopefuls, spring is in full bloom in Lexington.

Summer 36

Mid-season in the world of Lexington is a time of settling down to a new rhythm of life. Jacobson and the other parks bustle with picnics, skaters, and sun worshippers.

Fall 54

Lexington reaches its peak of seasonal glory when the fields of burley have turned to gold. If spring opened with a burst of seasonal glory, then fall becomes one of its great expectations.

Winter 74

No matter the weather, winter is the season when many church agendas will be as crowded with basketball events as if they were a part of the religious ritual itself.

COVER PHOTO BY JEFF ROGERS

PHOTOGRAPHY ON THE FOLLOWING PAGES BY JEFF ROGERS
13, 16, 37, 75, 92-93, 94, 122, 133

PHOTOGRAPHY ON THE FOLLOWING PAGES BY PAT MCDONOGH
2, 4-5, 8-9, 10, 12, 14-15, 54, 101, 121, 141, 142, 154, 160

Part Two

MANUFACTURING & DISTRIBUTION 94

BUSINESS, FINANCE, DEVELOPMENT & THE PROFESSIONS 100

THE EQUINE INDUSTRY ...122

HEALTH CARE 132

EDUCATION & QUALITY OF LIFE, HOSPITALITY & TOURISM 142

Foreword

Ours is a truly magnificent moment in time. Lexington is confidently and boldly engaging the opportunities and obstacles of the new century. A community greater than the sum of our parts, we are building a modern city of the global economy while preserving the traditions and landscape that serve as our signature.

The Jewel of the Bluegrass, Lexington is a community in which the natural beauty of our region is exceeded only by the potential of our people. The university that anchors us is poised to harness our abundance of intellectual capital, lifting our spirits and standard of living to an even higher plateau.

We stand at the threshold of a cultural renaissance. Our downtown is emerging as a vigorous center of commerce and culture: a place where artisans proudly display their wares, where business people make deals, where the young and young at heart enjoy numerous entertainment options.

A renewed sense of purpose and ambition permeates the atmosphere of our community, with new leaders emerging in business, government, education, and civic life. We are a community that couples a profoundly modern optimism for the future with a genuine appreciation of our ancient traditions.

It is our sincere hope that *Seasons of Lexington* adequately captures the essence of our community. As you look through this book it will become readily apparent that Lexington is among the best places in the world to raise a family, work, play, or visit. We hope you enjoy the tour.

—*Greater Lexington Chamber of Commerce*

Great Expectations

by Dr. Thomas Clark

The name "Lexington" in Kentucky is synonymous with that of the western frontier. Located well beyond the western rim of the Appalachian highlands, and in the midst of a fabulously fertile land, the town early became the hub of Kentucky commerce and society. The town's founders focused their attention on the land rather than on a navigable stream and the area snuggled between the forks of the Elkhorn Creek at once revealed itself as a new Eden. Remarkably, the gestation period of Lexington was short, and its earliest dawning vague. Sometime in an unrecorded past, Indian tribes found the land, and later a Euro-trader gathered knowledge of the rich meadow. The legend, in time, was strengthened by visitations of French, British, and even colonial traders and wanderers.

In the moment of mid-eighteenth century trade rivalries and rising land speculative fever, the Bluegrass west became a magic start of beckoning. In Charlottesville, Virginia, the Loyal Land Company was formed to promote exploration and claiming of broad areas of western lands. Heading a survey party, Dr. Thomas Walker led the way down the great buffalo-Indian trail into the declivity in the eastern rock face of the Appalachians. Standing in Cumberland Gap in mid-April 1750, Dr. Walker made note of his party's passing that day and went on toward the legendary meadowlands, but his ambition was thwarted by terrain and physical exhaustion.

For a quarter of a century, all but nameless parties of hunters and wanderers visited the western country. In the later years, there appeared among them the legendary frontiersmen Daniel Boone, Simon Kenton, and James Harrod, the doughty Virginian who made the first settlement in the western country with a land hunting party in 1774. Beginning the following year, there trailed into Kentucky a seemingly endless procession of emigrants. Harrod's fort became a point of departure for land hunters.

The historical, economical, and forthcoming political patterns and future mores of the rising town of Lexington were set by the lay and nature of the land itself. When Robert Patterson in 1779 built his cabin on the bank of Town Branch, he marked the beginning of the town of Lexington. He could not possibly have known that at the end of the Revolutionary War there would flow into Kentucky a stream of settlers, many of whom would make their homes around the site of his cabin. The newcomers arrived with their pockets stuffed with land warrants, and their hearts set on entering the new Eden.

Over two and a quarter centuries, the economic fortunes of Lexington have hinged on the turnings of the seasons and the land. From that nostalgic moment when the pioneers arrived in the Elkhorn country driving horse and cattle herds, flocks of sheep, and droves of hogs, much of the fortune of the Bluegrass was linked to the expanding cotton South. Field produce was drifted south by way of Kentucky River flatboats. Droves and flocks of animals were driven overland to markets as diverse as Baltimore and Mobile. In Lexington, the hempen rope and cotton baggage magnate, John W. Hunt, became Kentucky's first millionaire. There lingers in modern Lexington an essence of memory when

Cheapside Square was once a throbbing livestock market on court days, a time when thousands of farm animals were sold on those days to be driven overland to a broadly dispersed southern market. Livestock, hemp, tobacco, and grain were the very economic and cash flow blood of the Bluegrass.

From that moment when a huddle of frontier town trustees devised a lot and street town for what they believed would become Kentucky's central village, down to the raising of the last multi-storied office building astride Town Creek, Lexington has been a "sporting town." Horse races were run down its streets, and knife-throwing frontiersmen engaged in the sport of throwing "long bullets" to the consternation of many of its citizens. Mixed in with the first advertisements in the pioneering *Kentucky Gazette* were notices of the standing of named stallions. The horse, as much as Lexington's famous lawyers and politicians, was to become and remain a basic symbol of the region. The racetrack was as much an institutional landmark as the portals of Morrison Hall in Transylvania University.

In time, the University of Kentucky, along with other schools, were to all but function to the rhythms of a dribbled basketball. The passion for sports ranges from the seasonal crowdings into the stands of Keeneland Race Course or the trotting horse Mecca "The Red Mile," to ice hockey, baseball, and the Saturday night tobacco barn hide-away cockfights. One might venture historically and say that the sporting mania that grips the region is the last purely frontier trait that is discernible in modern-day Lexington.

During the decades of the latter part of the twentieth century, two events pushed Lexington far out beyond its frontier and agrarian moorings. The first was the initial stage of creating a cosmopolitan community by the decision of the Internal Business Machine Corporation (IBM) to move its corporate operation from Syracuse, New York, to Lexington. Never in the history of the town had there been such an inflow of new population, which wrought so many economic and social changes. The gates were opened to other industrial and human migrations. The second event was the revolutionary political pattern-breaking of the provincial Kentucky political system of county-urban separation. On January 1, 1974, there was placed in operation the Lexington-Fayette Urban County Government. The merger greatly enlarged the areas for more modernized planning and administration.

No matter the changes, the community astraddle the Town Creek has a magical power of attraction. The roads that feed into the central hub are daily sparkled with the solid phalanx of the lights of automobiles and pickup trucks that bring the army of workers from miles surrounding Lexington. Overhead, the hospital helicopters roar away bearing the critically ill, the victims of accidents, and others to the maze of hospitals. Despite it all, there drifts the tender memories and nostalgia of when Main Street was a veritable artery of human associations, the warehouses annually stuffed with baskets of golden burley leaves, and many of the Bluegrass stable horses better known to a wider public than the Governor in Frankfort.

BALL HOMES/DONAMIRE FARM

$\mathcal{B}$all Homes is a family institution, incorporated in Kentucky in 1959 by Don and Mira Ball of Lexington. Since its inception, Ball Homes has been a consistent leader in the Central Kentucky home building market, having built more than 680 homes in a single year and literally thousands of homes in neighborhoods across Central Kentucky. Looking to the future, Ball Homes will meet the needs of the ever-changing Central Kentucky housing market. With strong community partnerships and a strong work ethic, Ball Homes is able to provide quality housing at an affordable price.

In addition to establishing a thriving home building business, Don and Mira Ball own and manage their own Thoroughbred horse farm. Appropriately named "Donamire," the farm takes its name from a combination of Don and Mira's first names. The Ball family maintains their support of the industry that gives the Bluegrass its worldwide appeal, horse racing, and will provide good homes to those other Lexington residents, Thoroughbred horses.

DON JACOBS

In 1970, Don Jacobs converted a farm implement/hardware store into what would become a lifelong family business. That year, he opened his namesake car dealership, Don Jacobs Oldsmobile.

It wasn't long before Jacobs saw an opportunity to diversify. He added the Honda line to his inventory and later the BMW and Volkswagen lines. In addition to Don Jacobs' successful car dealerships, the company boasts a highly skilled service department, body shop, and parts department.

Don Jacobs' ability to recognize and hire good people is a part of its history and is the cornerstone for its future growth. To keep the company strong, Don Jacobs will provide its staff with specialized training, adhere to sound business principles, and rely on good, old-fashioned common sense. Most of all, the management and staff will uphold one simple concept: to treat others as they would like to be treated.

Part One

Spring

When the Great Meadow surrounding Lexington suddenly turns to a seamless carpet of green, when mares and foals are turned out to bask lazily in the sun, and when the ancient road past Henry Clay's Ashland becomes a shady bower nestled beneath the foliage of ash and oak trees, and the last basketball has been dribbled, and the Keeneland Race Course has become host to a new crop of Derby hopefuls, spring is in full bloom in Lexington.

*L*exington is known as the "Horse Capital of the World," and one only has to look around to know why. Throughout spring, long-legged thoroughbred foals dot the pastures surrounding the city. Yet no matter what month in which it is born, each thoroughbred foal shares the same first birthday of January 1 of the next year. Later, as the colt or filly grows, it will most likely come to know Keeneland Race Course, either by being sold as a yearling or two-year-old at one of the famous Keeneland sales or by racing down the dirt track in a future meet. It is in Lexington that these thoroughbred horses are bred, born, registered, and sold, and it is in Lexington that, eventually, many of the great racing horses are retired and buried. Regardless of a colt's future, it all begins in Lexington. PHOTOS BY JEFF ROGERS

*L*exington Cemetery, listed on the National Register of Historic Places, is not only the resting place of many famous individuals, but also a popular tourist attraction. Visitors to the Lexington area enjoy the beauty of flowering dogwood and magnolia trees, as well as almost 200 other species found on the grounds, along with two lakes situated amid lovely flower gardens with plants grown in the Cemetery's own greenhouse.

One of the most well-known figures buried in Lexington Cemetery is the Lexington politician, Henry Clay. While a historic marker is located on his grave, a 130-foot-tall monument with a statue of Clay faces his adored Ashland estate.

PHOTOS BY PAT MCDONOGH

A short distance from downtown is statesman Henry Clay's beautiful 20-acre wooded estate known as Ashland. Clay landscaped the gardens based on ideas he gathered on trips to England, and the current half-acre formal garden is meticulously maintained by the Garden Club of Lexington. Visitors can absorb the beauty of a wide variety of trees, shrubs, roses, and annuals, among other plants, while relaxing on a bench in the shade or painting a picture of the blooming irises.

(Opposite page) Lexington residents take advantage of the beauty of their peaceful neighborhoods with canopies formed by majestic Sycamore trees. At the same time, visitors find themselves exploring the Federal-style home of John Wesley Hunt, Kentucky's first millionaire. The Alexander T. Hunt Civil War Museum is located in this historic home and includes items relating to Confederate General John Morgan, Hunt's grandson. PHOTOS BY PAT McDONOGH

*T*here are so many interesting places in downtown
Lexington that can be enjoyed every day by residents and visitors.
Both Phoenix Park, with a plaza of fountain pools, and
Triangle Park, featuring a stepped wall of lighted, flowing water,
are favorite places for family, friends, and coworkers to gather
for a day's outing or a lunch break.

Not only do people stop by the urban parks, but they also can
tour the downtown historic neighborhoods such as Gratz Park.
Having housed Lexington's upperclass citizens in the 1800s,
today the area is a charming place in which to live, as well as a
scenic place in which to stroll.

Aside from parks and neighborhoods, the downtown area also
caters to arts and culture. The Lexington Children's Theatre,
which presents five plays throughout the school year at the
theatre, also has special functions and workshops to help
children explore their creativity. PHOTOS OPPOSITE PAGE BY PAT
MCDONOGH (TOP LEFT) AND JEFF ROGERS. PHOTOS THIS PAGE
BY PAT MCDONOGH

*E*ducation is a top priority for Fayette County, in which Lexington is located. With 50 elementary, middle, and high schools, an alternative school, and two applied technology centers, the County is committed to ensuring that each student receives the best education possible, and its dedication is rewarded with SAT and ACT scores consistently higher than the national averages. Most high school graduates pursue further education at one of the local colleges or universities near Lexington.

(Right) Located directly on the University of Kentucky's main campus, Lexington Community College (LCC) offers an open admission policy. Anyone with a high school diploma or GED certificate can attend LCC in order to obtain one of three associate degrees in Arts, Science, or Applied Science. The LCC campus provides an excellent quality of life through intramural sports, cultural events, and student organizations, to name a few.

(Opposite page) George Washington, Thomas Jefferson, John Adams, and Lexington's own Henry Clay are a few of the famous Americans that have been associated with Transylvania University since its founding in 1780 by a pioneering land company whose chief scout was Daniel Boone. Henry Clay not only served on the board of trustees, but he also was a law professor at Transylvania. Today, the University is committed to providing an excellent liberal arts education to its undergraduate students. Students on campus are encouraged to participate in activities such as politics, arts, fraternities, sororities, and other events including athletics. PHOTOS ON THIS PAGE BY JEFF ROGERS. PHOTOS ON OPPOSITE PAGE BY JEFF ROGERS (TOP) AND PAT McDONOGH

The Lexington Mounted Police Unit, founded in 1982 with four officers, patrols the downtown area of Lexington and has grown to include eight officers and a Sergeant. Although mounted officers' responsibilities are the same as other police officers, the unit specializes in crowd control and special events. The visibility from horseback allows one mounted officer to accomplish what 8 to 10 officers on foot can.

(Opposite page, above) Most of the research activities for the Department of Veterinary Science at the University of Kentucky are conducted at the Maxwell H. Gluck Equine Research Center. Established in 1987, this modern facility consists of well-equipped laboratories, animal care facilities, and a veterinary library. There also is an equine treadmill in the biomechanics/locomotion laboratory.

(Opposite page, below) Although real horses can be found throughout Lexington, visitors can easily become acquainted with racehorses in Thoroughbred Park. Seven life-size and realistic bronze racehorses thunder down the track with famous jockeys aboard, including Pat Day, Bill Shoemaker, and Jerry Bailey. Nearby, broodmares, foals, and the stallion, Lexington, have been "turned out" in the two and a half acre park situated at the east end of downtown.

PHOTOS BY JEFF ROGERS

Surrounding the city of Lexington are elaborate thoroughbred horse farms with rail fences and Bluegrass pastures, producing racing legends that have won Kentucky Derbys and Triple Crowns, and then have gone on to retire as studs and sire more legends. Local companies provide tours of many of these farms and their famous horses.

While many horses are bred to run under the owner's racing colors, many colts are bred to sell. Keeneland Race Course is well-known in the racing industry for its yearly sales of colts and broodmares. Buyers from all over the world attend in order to purchase future prospects for racing and other equine sports. These sales are open to the public sector, as well, and just recently, Keeneland implemented a sales program on the Internet.

The breeding, training, and racing of thoroughbreds is an extensive, involved industry. Farms employ numerous personnel to oversee the daily care of both the facilities and the animals. Stablehands maintain the stalls and barns while grooms and exercise boys—many of which are females—condition the horses in preparation for racing careers. Photos this page by Pat McDonogh (top and bottom) and Jeff Rogers. Photo opposite page by Jeff Rogers

*B*efore the start of the spring meet at Keeneland, entries are paraded around the paddock in front of spectators, as well as trainers, grooms, and owners. Keeneland's paddock area is unique in several ways. Not only is it beautifully landscaped with oaks, sycamores, and maples, but it is one of the few racetracks in the country that allows spectators to view the racehorses this closely. Once mounted, the jockeys and their horses are escorted to the track by outriders where the thoroughbreds are loaded into the starting gate.

(Opposite page, above) Keeneland is a great place for families to have an outing or learn more about horses, and those of all ages are invited to visit the facilities at the racetrack. Although Keeneland does not offer tours, visitors may explore the grounds with private guides, watch early morning workouts, and dine in the excellent restaurants. Children are welcomed year-round, but Saturdays during the meets are particularly fun for young ones as they enjoy breakfast in the Equestrian Dining Room followed by special equine demonstrations in the paddock areas.

(Opposite page, below)The anticipation of a race is heightened by the well-known sound of the bugle. Even those who are not horseracing fans recognize the refrain. At Keeneland, George "Buckey" Sallee is a familiar face as he delivers "The Call to Post" before a race.

(Following page) The thunder of the hooves is dimmed only by the screaming of the owners, trainers, and fans as a pack of horses, barely distinguishable from each other due to the track mud, heads out of the final turn and enters into the homestretch. All of the preparation, training, and final words of advice come down to no more than a neck, a nose, or the wire.

PHOTOS BY PAT MCDONOGH

Mid-season in the world of Lexington is a time of settling down to a new rhythm of life. Nearby, the fields of burley tobacco have become corduroy rows of promise. Jacobson and the other parks bustle with picnics, skaters, and sun worshippers. The Lexington Ballet, theatrical groups, and the annual Arts Festival gather in Woodland Park to enliven the tempo of the season. Almost as a grand finale, the Junior League's horse show gives an impressive climax to a fading summer.

Summer

In the state of Kentucky, there are more than one million acres of wildlife management areas. The Lexington region is privilege to state parks and national preserves that offer miles of hiking trails and a vast number of waterways—Kentucky has more than any other state in the continental United States. There are also 200 native species of fish—40 of which are game fish. PHOTO BY JEFF ROGERS

(Above) Greenspace is a common sight both in and around Lexington, but just as familiar are horses of all shapes and sizes. From area farms to the Kentucky Horse Park to Keeneland thoroughbreds to the mounted police, horses of all breeds can be viewed, petted, and admired by the public. PHOTO BY PAT MCDONOGH

*A*rts and culture can be found throughout Lexington in a variety of places including museums and galleries, which present well-known works of art, and parks, which display life-size statues and sculptures as found in Gratz Park. Aside from these, Lexington also proudly showcases the works of central Kentucky artists at ArtsPlace. This multi-purpose arts center features changing exhibits and is the site of free music and dance performances throughout the year.

(Below) Expounding on this local pride in art and in equines, the Lexington Arts & Cultural Council (LACC) presented a unique exhibit in the Summer of 2000. The event, entitled Horse Mania, was an exciting and fun project that took art to a new level. People who normally might not be inclined to visit a museum or gallery were afforded the opportunity to view art from a new perspective. Eighty extravagantly painted fiberglass thoroughbred horses stood majestically on the sidewalks of downtown Lexington from July 1 to November 15. Later these works of art were auctioned off to individuals and organizations with proceeds benefiting LACC's public arts fund and a variety of charities. PHOTOS BY JEFF ROGERS

*W*hile Lexington is a growing city, it retains a feeling of community with the convenience of a thriving downtown area in the midst of a burgeoning urban area. Residents of Lexington have a choice of housing from apartment complexes to historic districts to planned neighborhoods. And while the city is centrally located within a day's drive of two-thirds of the population in the United States, the city and surrounding areas have much to offer.

(Opposite page, above) The downtown area is a vital component in maintaining the city's cultural life through the arts and boasts a myriad of opportunities. The 1887 Lexington Opera House, restored to its original splendor in 1975, is just one example of the city's dedication to arts and culture. Today, the Opera House is host to ballet and stage performances, as well as some of the Lexington Philharmonic concerts.

(Opposite page, below) The Lexington Art League also is active in promoting the arts through exhibitions and education, along with membership and advocacy. While the League sponsors exhibits at several area locations, its headquarters are located at Loudoun House. Built in 1852, and listed on the National Register of Historic Places, Loudoun House is one of only five remaining castellated gothic villas in the United States. PHOTOS BY JEFF ROGERS

$\mathcal{T}$he quality of life in Lexington encompasses those of all ages and interests. The Lexington-Fayette Urban County Government's Division of Parks and Recreation operates more than 3,000 acres of parks, playgrounds, swimming pools, and golf courses, and it organizes an array of activities and events held at the county's 87 parks and five public golf courses.

Whether for charity or recreation, anyone who enjoys golfing will find just the course they are seeking in the Lexington area. Due to the mild winter weather and convenient location, Lexington's championship courses attract players from many other states who enjoy year-round games on both public and private courses.

(Above) After almost 50 years, the city of Lexington was proud to be selected as the home of a new professional baseball team named the Lexington Legends. Taking to the field from April through September, the Legends draw fans from throughout Kentucky to the spectacular new stadium, Applebee's Park, which offers amenities from luxury suites to a supervised children's play area. A combination lending to the perfect family outing. PHOTOS BY JEFF ROGERS

For nearly a century, the Bluegrass Airport has served Lexington in some capacity. From the early charter services out of Halley Field and Cool Meadow Airfield to its role providing supplies and equipment during World War II out of the municipal facilities constructed at Blue Grass Field, the airport has contributed to the growth and vitality of the area. Today, Bluegrass Airport serves Lexington commuters with daily flights on several commercial airlines. PHOTO BY JEFF ROGERS

Established in 1877, Saint Joseph Hospital has the distinction of being the first facility in Central Kentucky to perform open-heart surgery in 1959. The hospital has a cardiothoracic unit and a coronary care unit, as well as the Cancer Center and Saint Joseph Sleep Disorders Center, and it provides helicopter transportation to patients in eastern Kentucky. PHOTO BY JEFF ROGERS

Offering a complete choice of health care options, Lexington provides its residents with the best treatment possible from minor injuries at one of its dozen or so walk-in clinics to individualized care at one of five specialty hospitals. Local facilities provide both inpatient and outpatient care with services involving mental health, reconstructive surgery, physical therapy, neonatal and maternity care, open heart surgery, and numerous other precise procedures. PHOTO BY JEFF ROGERS

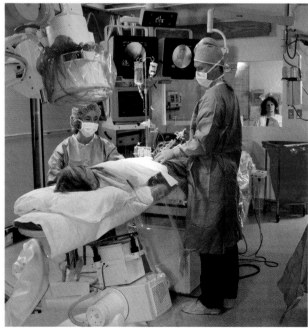

To see a world of horses in one place, horse enthusiasts have only to spend some time at the Kentucky Horse Park. Greeted by a statue marking the grave of the famous thoroughbred, Man o' War, visitors can view more than 40 breeds of resident horses and visit onsite museums, galleries, or theaters. The more than 1,000-acre park can be toured by a horse-drawn streetcar, carriage, or a ride on horseback. Throughout the year, horse shows featuring many different breeds and disciplines are held in the park's extensive facilities including the indoor arena, steeple-chase course, polo fields, and numerous dressage and show rings. PHOTOS BY JEFF ROGERS

*L*exington's oldest existing racetrack and one of the nation's most respected harness racing tracks, The Red Mile is home to live racing twice a year of trotters and pacers, known as Standardbreds. Open to the public year-round and offering intertrack waging, Red Mile is named for the clay soil of its track. It is home to the Grand Circuit Meet in the fall, the Kentucky Futurity, the third and final race in the Triple Crown of harness racing.

(Opposite page) Raising champions involves much more than the maintenance and growth of the horses. In order to maximize their animals' career potentials, breeding farms construct facilities to encompass every aspect of a horse's development and training including automatic walkers, therapeutic treadmills, and private tracks. PHOTOS BY JEFF ROGERS

*A*side from sporting events and parks, travelers to Lexington can enjoy other outdoor activities in Kentucky's welcoming climate. The Farmer's Market, which is open several days a week from spring until fall, is a fun place for Lexingtonians and visitors to shop for fresh fruits and vegetables sold by local farmers. The market also offers a variety of beautiful flowers and plants.

Bluegrass music is synonymous with Bluegrass Country. Although bluegrass music can be heard throughout Kentucky at different times of the year, one of the biggest events in the Lexington area is the Kentucky Bluegrass Festival held annually each June at the Kentucky Horse Park. This four-day event filled with family entertainment features talented bluegrass musicians carrying on a tradition and passing on a heritage. PHOTOS BY JEFF ROGERS

(Opposite and following page) Southwest of Lexington is a way of life that almost has been forgotten. Situated in the pastoral setting of Pleasant Hill, Kentucky, is Shaker Village. Established in 1805, the community thrived for a century while the people lived a simple, practical lifestyle. After the industrial revolution, the village all but disappeared until a nonprofit group was formed in the 1960s to restore and preserve a colony that may have had different beliefs from many, but managed to produce innovative ideas and inventions—the flat broom being the most well-known. Today, this National Historic Landmark is again thriving. Although the Shaker people no longer make their home here, visitors can learn about their way of life through the people of Shakertown who spin, weave, and make brooms just like it was a hundred years ago. PHOTO BY PAT McDONOGH (TOP) AND JEFF ROGERS. PHOTO ON FOLLOWING PAGE BY PAT McDONOGH

Fall

When the world tilts into its seasonal orbit, the

sun at eveningtide seems almost to sweep the treetops.

Lexington reaches its peak of seasonal glory when the

fields of burley have turned to gold, and the fall race meet

is in full swing at Keeneland. The universities bring

cities of students back to Lexington, and the course

of life is set to the beat of a more exciting drum.

If spring opened with a burst of seasonal glory,

then fall becomes one of its great expectations.

A short drive outside of Lexington are areas rich in history, including Old Fort Harrod State Park in Harrodsburg. James Harrod established this pioneer fort in 1774—the first permanent English settlement west of the Allegheny Mountains. The cabins located on the property display authentic pioneer furniture while craftspeople demonstrate daily chores. PHOTO BY PAT McDONOGH

(Opposite page) The beauty of nature surrounds the jockeys and horses that anxiously parade to the track where they will race against the best at Keeneland's fall meet, which is the final preparation for the championship Breeders' Cup. PHOTO BY JEFF ROGERS

Tobacco continues to be a mainstay of Lexington and Kentucky's financial system as it has for more than 200 years. For the colonists, tobacco was an essential part of the economy in America as it was often used as money. Today, tobacco-farming families, which have existed for generations, still thrive even though many farmers have turned to new products and technologies to provide their incomes. Photo by Jeff Rogers

(Opposite page) Another big Kentucky commodity is bourbon, considering that 95 percent of America's only native alcoholic beverage is manufactured in the Bluegrass state. Bourbon distilleries have come a long way in the last one hundred years or more, but the secrets to making a fine bottle of bourbon have not changed. Buffalo Trace, north of Frankfort, grew to become one of America's leading distilleries under the guidance of Albert Bacon Blanton, also known as Colonel Blanton. Over the years, the distillery has been modernized so that 10,000 bottles of bourbon are filled per hour, but tradition remains in the smaller bottling house where "single-barrel" bourbons are filled and sealed by hand. Aside from Buffalo Trace, which offers tours, Labrot & Graham and Wild Turkey Distillery are two other well-known Kentucky distilleries outside of Lexington that are open to the public. Photos by Pat McDonogh

Lexington is dedicated to preserving the beauty and tranquility of a small town while providing residents with all the amenities of a larger metropolitan area. One can enjoy natural settings while walking through a serene neighborhood or admire the elegance of downtown buildings mixed with trees and flowers. PHOTOS BY PAT MCDONOGH

Visitors to downtown Lexington can enjoy the sights in a variety of ways, but one unique and popular way is by horse-drawn carriage. Proudly pulled by elegant Percherons and other equines, these carriages drive people throughout downtown to tour places such as Henry Clay's law office in Gratz Park. PHOTO OPPOSITE PAGE BY JEFF ROGERS

(Opposite page, below) Another common site to visit on the downtown tour is the historic home of Mary Todd Lincoln, First Lady to President Abraham Lincoln, where President Lincoln enjoyed reading from his father-in-law's vast collection of books while staying with Mary's parents. PHOTO BY PAT McDONOGH

(Above) Located just a mile from the courthouse, visitors can make a side trip from their downtown jaunt with a stop at Henry Clay's beloved home, Ashland. PHOTO BY PAT McDONOGH

Fayette County's commitment to student excellence is demonstrated by the continuous awards received by its teachers and programs. The goals of district schools include increasing the students' learning in the area of literacy and technology, and ensuring that 100 percent of students graduate. PHOTOS BY PAT MCDONOGH

(Opposite page) Once these Fayette County students graduate, they are then afforded the opportunity to further their education through one of several local colleges and universities. Students can obtain degrees in numerous associate and undergraduate programs or earn graduate degrees at Lexington Community College, The University of Kentucky, and Transylvania University, to name a few. PHOTOS BY JEFF ROGERS (LEFT). PHOTO BY PAT MCDONOGH (RIGHT)

*W*hether touring horse farms or taking a relaxing drive through the countryside, Lexington and the surrounding areas offer spectacular scenery. An early morning drive may encounter heavy mists floating across the pasturelands where trainers and horses have already begun the day's work, and the winding roads—known as pikes in Kentucky—lead travelers around picturesque mountains to breathtaking views of the Bluegrass country. PHOTOS BY PAT McDONOGH

Lexington's size and location make it an excellent place for residents and visitors alike. With a top-ranked police department and crime safety programs, neighborhoods provide an exceptional quality of life for people of all ages. Serving to enhance this quality of life, the county's extensive parks and recreation division maintains public facilities and areas for family outings, activities, and events.

(Above) People are not the only residents of the area that enjoy playtime. Thoroughbred foals take pleasure in romping through acres of Kentucky Bluegrass pastures, relishing in their freedom as they grow and develop before beginning their training for the track. PHOTOS BY PAT MCDONOGH

all is synonymous with pumpkins and hayrides, and Lexingtonians know how to do it right. Children can visit area farms with family or classmates and ride a wagon out to the fields to select a plump, orange pumpkin. Being located in horse country gives these children a special advantage—instead of their wagon being pulled by a noisy tractor, it is hitched to enormous draft horses just like in the pioneer days. PHOTOS BY PAT MCDONOGH

(Following page) The more recent tradition of riding wagons to pick pumpkins is only a small part of Kentucky customs. One of the greatest Kentucky heritages is rooted deep within Kentucky soil—religion. Founded on religion and grown around religion, the Lexington area is home to a number of religious sectors, and many of these sects along with numerous churches have established their place in local history. One of the most recognizable is Pisgah Presbyterian Church, founded in 1874 by Irish and Scottish settlers. Located on the scenic Pisgah Pike, the church is accented by a distinctive rock fence that was built with native limestone and laid without mortar. PHOTO BY JEFF ROGERS

No telling what the gods of seasons and weather

will bring Lexington during the gray months of an Ohio

Valley winter. One thing is certain, a newspaper

reporter will trap a wooly worm to predict whether it will

be mild or rugged as indicated by the width of the ring

on its back. No matter the weather, there will be those

three months when basketball becomes the insatiable

passion of the town. Winter is the season when many

church agendas will be as crowded with basketball events

as if they were a part of the religious ritual itself.

Winter

The beauty of Red River Gorge Geological Area, situated southeast of Lexington, is not dispelled under the ice of a winter's day. In warmer weather, the Gorge is alive with hikers and campers taking in the magnificent scenery along hundreds of miles of trails that travel the raging Red River, which is Kentucky's only National Wild and Scenic River.

(Above) Although racing activity is suspended during the winter months, Keeneland continues to offer top breeding stock and racing prospects to buyers at the January Horses of All Ages Sale, one of six yearly sales held at the racetrack. PHOTOS BY JEFF ROGERS

The excitement of the horse industry may slow down in the cold of winter, but farms are continuously managing their herds and tending to their needs so the animals will be conditioned for the coming spring.

(Above) Equine Biodiagnostics, Inc., housed on the University of Kentucky campus, specializes in diagnostic laboratory testing for veterinarians and other equine services. This laboratory, along with other departments at UK, is dedicated to the progression of technology and medicine for horses and equine-related industries worldwide. PHOTOS BY JEFF ROGERS

*W*hether a student of education or the arts, Lexington has something to offer people with diverse interests. Lexington is home to the largest public university in the state—the University of Kentucky (UK). Educating in excess of 24,000 students each semester, UK offers both undergraduate and graduate degrees in top-quality courses. The university also is home to the Wildcats athletic program that has excelled in numerous sports, most notably basketball. PHOTOS BY PAT McDONOGH

For people who wish to receive cultural polish or simply enjoy local productions, organizations in the Lexington area are host to yearly and seasonal events that attract large crowds. Lexingtonians are committed to preserving arts and culture through a full range of performing arts groups including the Lexington Ballet Company, the Ballet Theater of Lexington, the Lexington Philharmonic, and the Lexington Children's Theatre. In addition, the Thoroughbred Center (formerly the Kentucky Horse Center, now owned by Keeneland) brings in several national touring companies during the school year, providing cultural entertainment to children. PHOTO BY JEFF ROGERS

*S*ports enthusiasts find no limit to the exciting world of sports as the American Hockey League introduced the Kentucky Thoroughblades to Lexington a few years ago. Taking to the ice in the fall and winter at Rupp Arena, the Kentucky Thoroughblades became Lexington's first professional sports team. PHOTO BY BRECK SMITHER. COURTESY OF THE KENTUCKY THOROUGHBLADES. PICTURED IS DEFENSIVE PLAYER STEVE BANCROFT

(Opposite page, above) Though recently established, the University of Kentucky Basketball Museum has become a very popular attraction in a short period of time. Celebrating almost a century of UK basketball, this 10,000-square-foot facility offers interactive, high-tech exhibits, historical timelines, and artifact displays. PHOTO BY PAT MCDONOGH

(Opposite page, below) Celebrating almost one hundred seasons of a winning tradition, The University of Kentucky basketball team continues to be a phenomenon sweeping the state. Playing in Memorial Coliseum for 26 years, then on to the third largest basketball facility in the country, Rupp Arena, for the last 25 years, the UK team has had astounding winning seasons that have created a huge following of fans throughout Kentucky and beyond. PHOTO BY JEFF ROGERS

The Lexington Center Corporation, a not-for-profit corporate agency of the Lexington-Fayette Urban County Government, owns and manages Heritage Hall and Rupp Arena, as well as the historical Opera House. Host to sporting events, concerts, conferences, meetings, and a wealth of other activities, Lexington Center is an essential part of the area's business community. PHOTOS BY JEFF ROGERS

(Opposite page) Lexington is a shopper's paradise boasting the second largest mall in Kentucky, and, whether a bargain hunter or antique dealer, shoppers can find whatever it is they need. From downtown Lexington to the suburbs, quaint shops and stores sell wares including handmade jewelry, pottery, crafts, art, clothing, and much more.
PHOTOS BY PAT MCDONOGH

From fine dining on the cuisine of world-renowned chefs to the simple tasting of local favorites at cozy eateries, Lexington dining is an experience in itself. Any palate can be satisfied with a casual lunch or a gourmet meal, with choices from barbecue to German to Japanese to pizza.

(Opposite page) From economy to luxury, whether filling room service orders or catering a large function, Lexington area hotels can oblige businessmen or conferences, families or family reunions.
PHOTOS BY JEFF ROGERS

*M*useums of all varieties can be found in Lexington. The Lexington Children's Museum features "hands-on" exhibits located throughout seven galleries. These presentations range from nature, to the human body, to world geography and culture, to archaeology, as well as information on Lexington history.

The Aviation Museum of Kentucky explores the history of flight through exhibits including ten airplanes from the 1920s to the present, as well as displays of engines, propellers, and historical information along with interactive exhibits. PHOTOS BY PAT McDONOGH

(Opposite and following page) As Lexington progresses into a new century and millennium, it never forgets those people who stood by their beliefs and led Kentucky to become the healthy, prosperous state it is today. By supporting museums and other preservation organizations, citizens can ensure that historians such as Henry Clay, John Morgan, and John Breckenridge are remembered for their contributions to the city of Lexington, today and in the future. PHOTOS BY JEFF ROGERS

Part Two

Manufacturing &
Distribution

GENERAL RUBBER AND PLASTICS COMPANY, INC.

In the late 1970s, Central and Eastern Kentucky's booming manufacturing, construction, and coal mining industries created new opportunities for a variety of suppliers in the area. As these industries grew, small industrial distributors began emerging all over the region.

18,000-square-foot Lexington facility. PHOTO BY STEWART BOWMAN

David Stone was working at an industrial distributor in Louisville when he recognized the enormous growth in Central and Eastern Kentucky. He began taking a closer look at Lexington, the state's second largest city, for a new venture. Not only was this city attractive because of the business opportunities it presented, its central location and high quality of life also peaked Stone's interest. So much so that in September of 1978, he and his family relocated to Lexington and opened General Rubber and Plastics.

The small industrial distributor began with three employees and a 4,800-square-foot facility in North Lexington. Although still situated at the same location, General Rubber and Plastics now boasts 50 employees and has expanded its Lexington facility to 18,000 square feet. The company leases an additional 16,000 feet of warehouse space nearby and now has offices in Eastern and Northern Kentucky.

General Rubber and Plastics sells manufacturing and packaging products from some of the world's most notable vendors, many of which are Fortune 500 companies. Goodyear, 3M, Rubbermaid, and General Electric adorn their impressive list of vendors.

The company's client list is just as impressive, serving national and international manufacturers such as Toyota Motor Manufacturing, Lexmark International, Trane Air Handling Systems, and Link-Belt Construction Equipment Company.

Although a main thrust of their business, General Rubber and Plastics does not stop at simply supplying manufacturing and packaging products to their customers. They are also problem-solvers, assisting their customers with streamlining and improving manufacturing processes. Over the years, customers have come to rely on the company's expertise to help increase productivity and offer higher quality products.

Stone attributes his company's success to being customer-service oriented and offering high quality products at competitive prices. He considers the company's competitive advantage to be their genuine concern for the customer and their needs, no matter the size or scope.

Customers continually recognize the company for their high quality approach to customer service. In 1999, Hitachi Automotive Products presented General Rubber and Plastics with a "Partnership in Quality" award for "distinguished achievement in the areas of quality, delivery, performance, customer management, and dedicated support." The company also helps its customers become recognized internally. Toyota's "Kaizen" program awards employees for improving quality or lowering product cost and it is through the assistance of General Rubber and Plastics that many of these awards are presented.

From day one, General Rubber and Plastics has embraced new technological advances in their industry and plans to keep the pace with these advances in the future. Although use of the Internet as an alternative way to communicate with customers is commonplace, the company will continue to focus on personal, face-to-face contact with customers and emphasize customer service as its highest priority. •

An employee operates a production saw for cutting plastics. PHOTO BY STEWART BOWMAN

THE VALVOLINE COMPANY

In the 1860s, when British scientist Dr. John Ellis found that crude oil had no medicinal purpose, he looked for an alternative use for the substance. Little did he know that he would uncover a use for oil that would revolutionize transportation and help build a new world economy.

Dr. Ellis proved the worth of crude oil by lubricating the valves in steam engines, one of the most significant means of power for transportation at that time. First known as The Continuous Oil and Refining Co., The Valvoline Company opened on September 6, 1866 in Binghamton, New York. Two years after the name "Valvoline" was coined, from the word "valve," signifying the company's strong relationship to the steam engine valve, the company was renamed "Valvoline Oil Company."

Valvoline became a part of its current parent company, Ashland Inc., in 1949 through a merger with the booming Ohio valley oil refiner. Valvoline moved its headquarters from Ashland, Kentucky, to Lexington in 1980, bringing 150 employees and their families to Bluegrass country. Lexington's relatively close proximity to the city of Ashland, its thriving economy, beautiful countryside, good educational system, and high quality of life made the city an attractive location for Valvoline to settle in and grow.

Now, the Lexington facility boasts 850 employees at its impressive campus in southeast Lexington. Four hundred of these employees work exclusively for Valvoline brands and the remaining 450 work for other Ashland divisions. Throughout its long and storied existence, Valvoline has been a leader in the lubrication, automotive service and automotive chemicals industries. Internationally renowned brands of products and services such as Valvoline, Eagle One, Zerex, SynPower, Pyroil, Premium Blue, Tectyl, and Valvoline Instant Oil Change are all managed from the Lexington headquarters.

Through encouragement of employee volunteerism and charitable contributions, Valvoline gives back to the community that has been so integral to its success. Since 1980, the company has become a significant contributor to local community service, arts, and civic organizations. Valvoline is the founding sponsor of the state's popular Bluegrass State Games athletic competition, which attracts thousands from all over the state. Valvoline's United Way employee contribution program continues to grow by leaps and bounds, and the company matches total employee contributions each year.

New Valvoline MaxLife® Motor Oil is specially formulated for cars with more than 75,000 miles.

Of course, Valvoline cannot be mentioned without noting its involvement in motor racing. Valvoline and auto racing have become synonymous, and there is an obvious excitement and pride in Valvoline's home office as a big race approaches. In 2001, Valvoline made history as the first major consumer products company to both own and sponsor a NASCAR Winston Cup racing team.

In 1999, Valvoline started a "Caring Hands" program with Big Brothers Big Sisters of America. The goal of this program is to raise $1 million and recruit thousands of new volunteer Big Brothers and Sisters.

Valvoline is now pioneering an effort to produce higher quality, or "premium," automotive products that will improve automobile performance. The company prides itself on its ability to introduce new products in a timely fashion, and is continually changing its strategies to adapt to new market conditions. Valvoline will continue to be a responsible corporate citizen and community leader throughout the new millennium. •

Valvoline Instant Oil Change is one of America's leading fast oil-change service brands.

BAUMANN PAPER CO.

*I*n 1940, Fred Baumann, Sr. was working at Lexington's Phoenix Hotel when he overheard a hotel patron discussing an open sales position at his paper company in Cincinnati. At the time, Mr. Baumann was the chief buying steward in charge of purchasing paper and related products for the historic hotel. He stepped forward and told the man that he would be interested in working part-time and was hired on the spot.

After World War II, the paper product business was booming and Mr. Baumann saw the potential for growth in the Central Kentucky market. Since his boss was not interested in his proposal, he decided to strike out on his own. Baumann Paper Company was begun March 1, 1950 in the basement of the Baumann home. Mr. Baumann's wife and next door neighbor became the first two employees of the business, working as secretaries for the company. The garage was used as a warehouse.

Growth came quickly and it was not long until Baumann Paper Company moved out of its humble home and rented space in a warehouse at on Main Street in downtown Lexington. In 1969, an opportunity to buy a facility came along, which meant yet another move for the company. The company moved to Manchester Street and converted a 65,000-square-foot tobacco warehouse to the warehouse and offices for the growing company. After operating for seven years there, growth again sparked the need for a larger facility and, in 1976, Baumann Paper Company bought an 80,000-square-foot building and moved into it three years later.

Today, Baumann Paper Company is led by Fred Baumann, Jr., who started working for his father at the age of 13. Approximately 50 work in sales, clerical, warehousing, and delivery for the company.

Hiring and retaining quality employees who view their positions as "careers," not just as jobs has been a key for success to Baumann Paper Company. PHOTO BY DAVID COYLE

For years, Baumann Paper Company has been the only industrial paper company in central Kentucky. But don't let the name deceive you—Baumann Paper Company sells much more than just paper products. Products made from plastic, foam, and foil are among the company's large catalog of items sold to healthcare, foodservice, laundry, office building, industrial, lodging, grocery, and retail operations statewide and regionally.

Mr. Baumann credits his company's success to offering quality products at competitive prices with on-time delivery. Providing five-day-a-week delivery is no longer a luxury for customers, but a requirement for paper product distributors. Hiring and retaining quality employees who view their positions as "careers," not just as jobs has also been key for success. Baumann maintains a competitive edge by staying on the cutting edge of technology and being astute to rapidly changing environmental issues.

Baumann Paper Company is prepared for the challenges of the future. As technology and e-commerce become more utilized, Baumann will respond by making its products available through whatever means the customer desires. As it has for the past 50 years, Baumann Paper Company will adapt to the changing market conditions and provide the highest quality products, on time, at competitive prices. •

Providing five-day-a-week delivery is no longer a luxury for customers, but a requirement for paper product distributors. PHOTO BY DAVID COYLE

THE TRANE COMPANY

he Trane Company traces its roots to a plumbing company started by James Trane, a Norwegian immigrant, in LaCrosse, Wisconsin in 1885. Not long after the company's incorporation in 1913, Trane expanded his business to include the up-and-coming climate control trend of that era—heating. By 1916, the company abandoned plumbing altogether to take advantage of the high demand for climate control processes and systems.

In 1925, Trane came up with a revolutionary new idea that would prove to be a tremendous technological improvement in the industry and would lead to the modernization of heating and ventilating equipment manufacturing. This new idea resulted in the development of a simple coil, through which steam or hot and cold water could pass. The tightly bonded coil greatly improved the transfer of heat and cold and became the basic component for many of the heating and cooling products manufactured in the 1920s and '30s. Today, The Trane Company manufactures a variety of heating and cooling units, each of which still use the Trane coil as its primary element.

The Lexington facility is the 2nd largest Trane Manufacturing Plant under one roof. PHOTO BY STEWART BOWMAN

The Trane Company is still headquartered in LaCrosse, Wisconsin. This home base employs most of its development, research, and manufacturing engineers and administrative personnel. There are plants in a number of other cities across the nation, as well as internationally. In 1984, The Trane Company became a wholly-owned subsidiary of American Standard, Inc., a Fortune 500 company that is listed on the New York Stock Exchange.

In the 1960s, as transportation became increasingly important to manufacturers, The Trane Company chose to construct a manufacturing facility and office building in Lexington. Built in 1963, this site was selected for its central location to major markets and close proximity to Lexington's perimeter belt-line highway, providing easy access to carriers who can skip inner city congestion and provide better delivery and shipping schedules to customers.

Today, the Lexington facility is the second largest Trane Manufacturing plant under one roof. Lexington's employees have enjoyed stable employment in a somewhat fluctuating economy since opening in 1963. This plant manufactures coils and air handling equipment. Most of these products are used in large commercial and industrial applications such as schools, churches, office buildings, and shopping centers.

What's unique about Trane's manufacturing capabilities is that most of its products can be customized specifically to a customer's needs. The company also prides itself on quick shipping cycles and on time delivery. And, Trane became ISO-9001 certified in 1999 and has adopted a company-wide vision for quality control.

Although one of the largest markets served by the Lexington plant is the heavily populated southeastern portion of the United States, products made in this facility bring comfort to people all over the world. Trane Air Handlers have been installed in such national landmarks at the Gateway Arch in St. Louis, Missouri, Fort Knox in Kentucky, and the Washington Monument.

Constant engineering changes, product improvements, and new product manufacturing have made The Trane Company what it is today. In challenging the future, the company is equipped with one of the most complete and steadily expanding product lines of environmental control equipment for air conditioning, heating, ventilating, and heat transferring. •

Products made in Trane's Lexington facility bring comfort to people all over the world. PHOTO BY STEWART BOWMAN

Business, Finance, Development & The Professions

BALL HOMES/DONAMIRE FARM

Ball Homes is a family institution, incorporated in Kentucky in 1959 by Don and Mira Ball of Lexington. Don, Mira and the second generation of the Ball family now operate the business: Ray Ball is the company's president, and Mike Ball and Lisa Ball Sharp are vice-presidents. As its name implies, Ball Homes specializes in the construction of single-family homes, but the company is involved in several aspects of Central Kentucky's housing market, including land development and property management.

Since its inception, Ball Homes has been a consistent leader in the Central Kentucky home building market, having built more than 680 homes in a single year and literally thousands of homes in neighborhoods across Central Kentucky. In the 1990s, the company expanded from its strong Lexington base to the surrounding communities of Versailles, Georgetown, Nicholasville, Midway, Paris, and Richmond. In 1997, Ball Homes moved into the competitive Louisville, Kentucky market. Quickly, the company grew its business in the Louisville market from nine initial homes in a single neighborhood to 200 homes in six neighborhoods by the year 2000. As a result of the company's steady growth over the decade of the '90s, Ball Homes was honored by *Builder Magazine* in 1998 and 1999 as one of the top 100 builders of single family homes in the nation.

Thoroughbred "Twilight Road." PHOTO BY STEWART BOWMAN

One of Donamire's Thoroughbreds. PHOTO BY DAVID COYLE

Ball homes can be spotted in such notable Lexington communities as Lake Crossing, Brighton Woods, Timber Creek, Willow Bend, and Canter field. In Lexington's surrounding towns, the company has built Hambrick Place and Bradford Place in Georgetown, as well as the Highlands in Paris and North Ridge in Midway. In Versailles, Ball Homes built the Lanes View neighborhood and, in Nicholasville, homes in the Southbrook, Orchard Pointe, and Brittany Pointe neighborhoods. Neighborhoods in Louisville that feature Ball homes include the Brooks of Hickory Hollow, Adams Run, Wolf Trace, Bay Tree Meadows, Breckinridge Meadows, the Hills of Beckley Station, the Reserve at Beckley Station, and the La Grange neighborhood of Woodland Lakes.

Once primarily a builder of starter homes, Ball Homes has grown to offer a diverse and increasing array of mid-sized floor plans and semi-custom homes. Many Ball Homes customers are repeat buyers whose housing needs have kept pace with the company's growth. These loyal customers enjoy the quality, value, and service represented in all Ball Homes and continue to find new locations and floor plans that suit their changing lifestyles. The company offers over forty floor plans, ranging in size from just over 1,000 square feet to nearly 3,000 square feet. In-house architects design many of Ball Homes' best-selling

View of training barn from across grass track and lake. Photo by David Coyle

floor plans, ensuring that the plans reflect the preferences of the local market. The numerous awards the company has won for its homes demonstrate their market appeal among homebuyers in the Central Kentucky market. The company has participated regularly in the Home Builders Association's Grand Tour of Homes and Parade of Homes events, winning nearly 40 "Best of Show" awards since 1989.

Ball Homes attributes much of its success to strong relationships with other home selling and building organizations. One such organization is Rector Hayden Realtors. Since 1990, Ball Homes has enjoyed a partnership with Rector Hayden in marketing all of their Lexington-area homes. Each local Rector Hayden office has a team of Ball Homes specialists devoted to representing the Ball Homes neighborhoods. In the Louisville area, a team of agents at the Brownsboro Road Prudential Parks and Weisburg office represent Ball Homes. These partnerships with well-established local real estate agencies give customers the benefits

Donamire's broodmare barn. Photo by Stewart Bowman

of having a large field of experts to help them shop for new homes, market their current homes, or work through the cumbersome relocation process.

Ball Homes also has a strong relationship with the Lexington Home Builders Association, as well as the state and national branches of that organization. As a "Registered Builder Member" of the Association, Ball Homes works closely with this trade association to advance affordable housing, continue the education of its membership, and maintain a high level of professionalism throughout the industry. Several Ball family members have served the Lexington association as president, and the company maintains memberships in the Scott County, Madison County, and Louisville branches of the Association.

Ball Homes enjoys another successful partnership with 2-10 Homebuyer's Warranty, a national company that provides an insured warranty for all new Ball homes. The insured warranty, which is locally administered and serviced by the builder, offers added assurance to the homebuyer. The Balls have been honored by the 2-10 company for Ball Homes' consistent service and customer satisfaction.

Success in a community such as Lexington can also be attributed to relationship building and community support. Ball Homes and the Ball family are proud supporters of such diverse organizations as the Hope Center, the Alzheimer's Association, the United Way, KET, the Lexington Opera House and the Humane Society. However, the Balls' greatest contribution to the Central Kentucky area over the past forty years is their commitment to affordable housing. The Balls are proud to promote home ownership for a diverse group of people in Kentucky, both through their own company's emphasis on moderately-priced homes, and through their community service interests.

In 1993, the family created Barkham, a non-profit construction firm that provides at-cost development, construction and remodeling services to worthy projects. Since its inception,

Weanlings graze near the broodmare barn. PHOTO BY STEWART BOWMAN

Barkham has built Virginia Place, a 56-unit one-parent apartment facility. Virginia Place, which includes a childcare facility and community building, is designed to help single-parent families acquire family life skills and achieve independent living. Barkham has also provided services for Lexington's Center for Training and Employment and the Kentucky Racing Health and Welfare Fund. Other Barkham projects include the Hope Center for Women, Shepherd's Place, and Serenity Place, all designed to work with Lexington's Hope Center in providing services and ongoing housing assistance for homeless men and women.

The Balls regularly build homes in conjunction with Habitat for Humanity, and are founding supporters of REACH, an organization whose work is to further the development of lower and moderate-income housing. In 1999, Don Ball was honored for the scope, duration, and impact of his community service

The formal garden at Don and Mira Ball's home includes a reflecting pool. PHOTO BY STEWART BOWMAN

with the Hearthstone Builder Lifetime Public Service Award, sponsored by the Hearthstone Foundation and *Builder Magazine*.

In addition to establishing a thriving home building business, Don and Mira Ball own and manage their own Thoroughbred horse farm. Appropriately named "Donamire," a combination of Don and Mira's first names, this 600-acre farm is located in the heart of Kentucky's horse country. The farm is comprised of five tracts of land that Don and Mira have acquired since 1980 when they moved their Thoroughbred operation from a nearby farm.

Donamire Farm is home to more than fifty Thoroughbred horses. While many Thoroughbred farms throughout Central Kentucky are strictly business operations, both Don and Mira Ball and their son Mike Ball's family reside there.

Donamire is perhaps most widely recognized for its picturesque stone barns with steeply pitched slate roofs, cupolas, and spires, set among miles of curving white fences that follow the contours of the rolling hills common to Kentucky's horse country. Footage from Donamire was taken for the feature film *Simpatico* and the "made-for-television" movie *A Horse for Danny*. The farm is open to guided tour buses and includes a scenic pull-off with a panoramic view of the training complex, track, and one of the property's four lakes.

The broodmare barn houses an average of a dozen mares in foal during the season, whose bloodlines include Alleged, Storm Cat, Sir Ivor, and Halo. Similar in architecture to the broodmare barn is the nearby yearling barn, where young horses are cared for and taught basic handling. The largest of Donamire's barns, the long training barn, overlooks a 5/8-mile dirt track that encircles a lake, and a one-mile grass track that also surrounds a lake. Here, Katherine Ball trains all of the farm's runners, who race locally at Keeneland, Churchill Downs, Turfway, and Ellis Park, as well as other racetracks across the country. Some of Donamire's most notable racehorses include Summer Advocate, Recusant, Going Straight, Going Investor, Grand Teton, Vite View, Ambassador's Image, and Suffragette.

The farm's office and residential buildings, designed by the Balls and

Lexington architect Thomas Lett, blend in style with the architecture of the Thoroughbred barns, with their arched windows, stone accents and steep roof lines. The farm office, which serves as Don Ball's business head-quarters, includes a formal terrace garden based on sketches by Frank Lloyd Wright. The farm office and lawns serve as a base for the many professional, civic, and charitable events hosted by the Balls.

Private riding facilities are based largely on a 300-acre section of the farm. A fourteen-stall riding barn, round pen, and regulation-size riding ring serve as the base for the family's collection of riding horses. The trails feature acres of open pasture and a series of private bridle paths that curve through wooded areas and border a branch of Lexington's beautiful North Elkhorn Creek.

But what is most special about Donamire Farm is its natural beauty. Extensive landscaping by the Balls compliments the mature burr oak, walnut trees, and tulip poplars that shade the fields. The Balls have planted hundreds of trees, including Ash, Sweetgum, and Maple that line the roadways with color in the fall. Springtime brings redbud, dogwood, and crabapple blossoms all over the farm and beds of tulips punctuate the roadside. A greenhouse conservatory overlooks a rock waterfall and day lily beds at the edge of the farm's largest lake. Future plans for the farm include a guesthouse and wine vineyard.

Donamire has historic appeal as well. One of the most historic aspects of Donamire is a section of a drystack limestone fence, constructed as many as 150 years ago by Irish stonemasons and refurbished in 1996 by a local stonemason. A spring-fed cistern in a large paddock was once a primary stopping place and watering

Fall color is part of Donamire's natural beauty. PHOTO BY DAVID COYLE

hole for travelers on horseback between Lexington and Kentucky's state capital, Frankfort.

Looking to the future, Ball Homes will strive to meet the needs of the ever-changing Central Kentucky housing market. With strong community partnerships and a strong work ethic, Ball Homes will continue its commitment to providing quality housing at an affordable price. The Ball family will maintain their support of the industry that gives the Bluegrass its worldwide appeal, horse racing, and will provide good homes to those other Lexington residents, Thoroughbred horses. •

The broodmare barn paddocks overlook the Old Frankfort Pike entrance to Donamire. PHOTO BY STEWART BOWMAN

DON JACOBS

In 1970, Don Jacobs converted a farm implement/hardware store into what would become a lifelong family business. That year, he opened his namesake car dealership, Don Jacobs Oldsmobile, near Lexington's old stockyards. The odds were against him. The longest strike in General Motors history was taking place and there hadn't been an Oldsmobile dealership in Lexington in over a year. Despite these unusual circumstances, that first year the auto dealership continually outsold both the local Buick and Pontiac dealerships, combined.

It wasn't long before Jacobs saw an opportunity to diversify. Just before a paralyzing gas shortage hit the U.S. in the early '70s, he added the Honda line to his inventory, a car line known for being fuel-efficient. This growth created a need for a larger facility. In 1974, a new 46,000-square-foot facility was opened on Nicholasville Road. At that time, this location

BMW 740i in imola red. PHOTO BY STEWART BOWMAN

was considered rural. Now, it lies at one of the busiest intersections in the state.

Growth prompted yet another construction project for Don Jacobs in 1985. The Honda line's success created a need for a facility of its own. That year, a 23,000-square-foot facility was built at the Nicholasville Road site.

Clean state-of-the-art service shop. PHOTO BY STEWART BOWMAN

In 1989, just as the "Baby Boomers" were either enjoying the fruits of their labor or simplifying their lives, Don Jacobs added the BMW and Volkswagen lines.

In addition to Don Jacobs' successful car dealerships, the company boasts a highly skilled service department, body shop, and parts department. The service department services cars of all makes and models, from imports to domestics. Three master manufacturer technicians, five ASE-certified master technicians, and other ASE-certified technicians assist customers with their vehicle needs and services. The well-equipped body shop repairs all types of body damage including major repairs, dents and dings, paint retouching, reapplication of pin striping, and complete paint jobs. The parts department carries an extensive inventory of parts in stock. Customers rarely endure the time-consuming parts ordering process.

Of course, no successful dealership would be complete without a full line of used cars. And Don Jacobs boasts the largest used car inventory in Central Kentucky. The dealership understands that different people have different tastes and different income levels. All of the company's pre-owned vehicles are taken through an extensive inspection and recon-ditioning process prior to sale.

Don Jacobs attributes much of its success to its ability to attract and retain quality employees. The employee roster has grown from around 20 in the early '70s to nearly 175 at the turn of the century. Don Jacobs prides itself on its specialized employee training program, both initially and on an on-going basis throughout an employee's career with the company. Employees participate in live, interactive satellite training seminars conducted by the dealership's manufac-turers. A well-stocked library of motivational and sales training books and materials is accessible by all employees.

Of course, Don Jacobs would be nothing without its customers. That is why special emphasis is placed on customer satisfaction. Don Jacobs has maintained one of the highest Customer Satisfaction Index ratings of any major dealer in the U.S. Customers from throughout Kentucky and the nation return time and time again to purchase automobiles from the dealership. Some as far away as New England and Florida have returned due to exceptional customer service.

Showrooms allow up to 20 vehicles on display. PHOTO BY STEWART BOWMAN

A few simple, yet very important, practices help ensure high satisfaction ratings. For example, every Don Jacobs customer is not only contacted the day after a vehicle is purchased, but as long as they own their car to gauge the customer's satisfaction level and to encourage feedback about the Don Jacobs buying experience. Every service customer is given a postage-paid survey card and encouraged to send the dealership feedback about their service experience.

Looking at the Don Jacobs logo, one might wonder why it features a large red apple. And those who purchase a vehicle from Don Jacobs might wonder why there is a big juicy red apple waiting in their new vehicle. The dealership likens the car-buying experience at Don Jacobs to eating a fresh, juicy apple. Simply put, it's sweet. That is the way the dealership would like to be remembered.

Don Jacobs gives back to the community that has supported it so well over the past three decades. Management and staff volunteer numerous hours to such charitable organizations as the Susan G. Komen Foundation (breast can-cer awareness), MADD, Kentucky Educational Television, Ashland, the Henry Clay Estate, and the United Way.

Don Jacobs's ability to recognize and hire good people is a part of its history and is the cornerstone for its future growth. To keep the company strong, Don Jacobs will provide its staff with specialized training, adhere to sound business principles, and rely on good, old-fashioned common sense. Most of all, the management and staff will uphold one simple concept: to treat others as they would like to be treated. •

Large indoor service reception area. PHOTO BY STEWART BOWMAN

OAK GROVE AT LEXINGTON

*A*partment living made elegant—that's how the apartment community of Oak Grove has been described since opening in Lexington in 1998. Oak Grove's 230 luxurious apartment homes, resort style features, and unmatched customer service have helped create an outstanding reputation in the community.

The warm colors of Oak Grove are enhanced by the changing leaves of fall. PHOTO BY DAVID COYLE

Lexington was handpicked as a site for the Schaedle Worthington Hyde (SWH) development. Rob Schaedle, a partner in SWH, is a horse owner and has a fond affinity for Lexington. Bob Worthington, also a partner in the Atlanta-based company, has family living in the area. These reasons along with a strong personal interest in the area led them to establish the Oak Grove community. In addition, Lexington had an obvious need for upper end apartment homes in the area making it the perfect site for an apartment community the caliber of Oak Grove.

SWH prides itself on uncompromising quality and professionalism in everything they do. The company believes that success as a developer and manager in today's multi-family housing market rests on an understanding of residents and their changing lifestyle needs. Innovative, luxurious apartment designs, and responsive residential services reflect the company's unrelenting commitment to the individuals and families who rent their homes. SWH communities are constructed with quality workmanship. Inside its apartments are floor plans the lend themselves to relaxing, entertaining, and enjoying hard-earned leisure time.

Oak Grove is no exception. One, two, and three bedroom homes ranging from 740 to over 1,200 square feet accommodate individuals, couples, or families. Each home features a private sundeck or sunroom. Nine-foot ceilings, tiled entries and oversize windows give each apartment home a house-like feel.

Conveniently located off Man O' War, Oak Grove's elegant buildings are nestled in the rolling landscape. PHOTO BY DAVID COYLE

Most homes feature several closets including walk-in, linen, coat, and storage closets. But what makes Oak Grove "luxurious" are some of the not-so-common features like textured walls, built-in bookcases, ceiling fans, brass chandeliers, and tiled fireplaces.

No upscale apartment community would be complete without a long list of property amenities. Oak Grove's list begins with a location that is quiet and convenient, and is within minutes of shopping, dining, and recreation opportunities. Electronically controlled entry gates enhance privacy and decrease traffic in and out of the community. Oak Grove's impressive grounds are out-lined in lush landscapes and meticulously maintained. A sparkling swimming pool and spacious sun deck are available to residents during the summer months and a fully equipped fitness center is accessible 24 hours a day. Even residents' cars are pampered with detached garages and a covered car wash bay and vacuum.

Although luxurious floor plans, home features and amenities are important to the success of an upscale apartment community, SWH believes putting residents first is the most important factor for success. The company approaches customer service differently than many of its competitors. For example, Oak Grove has a resident service team versus a hierarchy of apartment managers and leasing consultants. Each "resident service associate" is fully cross-trained to answer any and all questions from residents. That way, residents rarely have to wait for answers due to bureaucracy or misinformation. When a resident has a question, there should always be someone knowledgeable available to provide an answer.

The property guarantees 24-hour maintenance turnaround and strives for immediate response to emergency maintenance calls. Every resident is furnished with a list of home phone numbers for

Oak Grove's Apartment Homes offer residents a showcase to display their own sense of style. PHOTO BY STEWART BOWMAN

Richly appointed interiors make living grand. PHOTO BY DAVID COYLE

the property's resident service team, in case of an emergency and an emergency contact number is monitored 24 hours a day. So, if a resident's refrigerator goes out, for example, an Oak Grove team member immediately works on a solution to rectify the situation. Doing so decreases the inconvenience to the resident and gives immediate satisfaction.

But having knowledgeable employees and a responsive maintenance crew is considered elementary to Oak Grove's customer service effort. Instead of striving to provide what they would consider basic residential services, Oak Grove goes beyond the call of duty to understand residents' more intricate needs and to be accommodating to those needs. The mainte-nance supervisor helps with more than just

Stacked stone in warm earth tones grace the buildings at Oak Grove.
PHOTO BY STEWART BOWMAN

Residents aren't the only ones who appreciate Oak Grove's exceptional customer service efforts. The young Lexington property has received numerous industry awards, both locally and on the national level. The Lexington Apartment Association gave Oak Grove the "Best Overall Team" award during the 1999 Crowne Excellence Awards. In 2000, the Association recognized select team members as "Maintenance Supervisor of the Year," "Assistant Manager of the Year," and "Leasing Consultant of the Year." Oak Grove was also awarded "Best of Show" in 1999. On the national level, SWH was honored by CEL & Associates as among the best in the industry for customer satisfaction in the annual National Real Estate Customer Service Awards program. SWH conducts an awards program amongst its own properties each year and Oak Grove is always in the running for a major award. In 1999 and 2000, the property was given the "Purple Heart Award for Outstanding Customer Service." And, in 2000, Oak Grove was recognized as having the best customer service team in the east region, based solely on customer service responses.

In the fiercely competitive housing market, some might consider Oak Grove's attitude toward its competition a bit strange. Not only does the community encourage competition, Oak Grove prides itself on the positive working relationships it has developed with its competitors. For residents who are not in the market for an upscale apartment community, Oak Grove's friendly team willingly provides referrals to other local apartment communities. In turn, these properties do the same for Oak Grove.

To develop and manage successful apartment communities like Oak Grove, SWH operates under one simple concept: to simply be the best real estate company in the business, bar none.

major repairs, helping residents with simpler tasks like hanging pictures or programming a VCR. Not only is there a convenient clothes care center on site, the community offers a valet dry cleaning service. For out-of-town guests that cannot be accommodated by residents or who just need some privacy, a fully furnished guest suite is available on site. A book and video library is kept at the clubhouse and residents are encouraged to make recommendations for additions to the library's stock. Every weekday morning, a continental breakfast is served, providing a forum for residents to get to know team members and their neighbors. In the summer, cool refreshments are served poolside to swimmers and sunbathers. Oak Grove understands the importance of establishing a good first impression. That is why they give new residents extra special attention the day they move in, making the transition to their new neighborhood a pleasant one.

Bold architectural integrity and sophistication characterize every home. PHOTO BY DAVID COYLE

Style, elegance, and tradition. PHOTO BY STEWART BOWMAN

integrity, hard work, and achieving a high quality of life should be of the utmost importance.

Including Lexington's Oak Grove, to date SWH owns and manages more than 6,700 units of apartments and seven hotels located in 11 states and 20 markets throughout the eastern United States. The company owns and operates three divisions: development/acquisitions, construction, and management. SWH has main offices in Atlanta, Georgia, and Nashville and regional management offices in Greensboro, North Carolina, Memphis, Tennessee, and Birmingham, Alabama.

Schaedle Worthington Hyde Property Management fee manages for Northwestern Mutual Life, Clark and Clark, and MBKS in Tennessee, New York, and Colorado. The company uses state-of-the-art technology and software programs like CLR's Rent Roll and MAS90 accounting software. All of SWH's properties are linked to the home office with a remote electronic mail system.

With the guidance and support of Schaedle Worthington Hyde Properties, Oak Grove at Lexington has a bright future. With an emphasis on providing quality apartment homes and impeccable customer service, Oak Grove will continue to serve Lexington's upscale apartment home needs. •

At the heart of this concept is an overriding principle of leadership through service to its customers, owners, residents, clients, families, and communities. In an effort to be "the best," SWH consistently focuses on three main areas: value enhancement, individual achievement, and team cooperation. The company believes that to create the value necessary to ensure profitability for both the long- and short-term, they must pay diligent attention to the best financial interests of its owners, have a tireless commitment to quality apartment living, and provide for the well-being of employees. The company believes that employees are its greatest asset and works to make each employee a successful team member. Those employees who achieve success are assured recognition by SWH of their achievements. The company encourages its management teams to create a business environment that fosters individual entrepreneurship and informal, open management decisions. This environment should promote team spirit and mutual cooperation. Above all, honesty,

Oak Grove—southern elegance and community charm. PHOTO BY DAVID COYLE

GREATER LEXINGTON
CHAMBER OF COMMERCE

In 1881, Lexington was making a transformation from a small country town to a bustling metropolis. Across the country, "chambers of commerce" were being created to help perpetuate commerce for growing cities. That same year, Lexington was the next growing city to follow this trend with the creation of the Greater Lexington Chamber of Commerce.

View of Lexington skyline. PHOTO BY DAVID COYLE

Today, the Lexington Chamber is still dedicated to assisting businesses in the local area to succeed and grow. But businesses aren't the only community members benefiting from the Chamber's efforts. The scope of the Chamber over its long and storied past has changed from a barterer of business to a builder of the community. Although its focus is still economic growth and prosperity for Lexington, other "quality of life" elements receive attention from the Chamber like the environment, recreation, education, leadership, and government. Its goal is to be a positive community-change agent, forming partnerships between business, education, government, and others to build a stronger community with a higher quality of life.

A membership organization by nature, the Chamber assists over 2,000 members in becoming successful in Lexington's business community. The membership is a direct reflection of Lexington's business composition, with over 80 percent of members having fewer than 50 employees.

The inner workings of the Chamber include operations, public affairs and education, and marketing functions. The operations arm of the Chamber acts as a business manager, ensuring the Chamber attracts high quality staff members, elects strong leaders for its board of directors, and plans strategically and responsibly for the future. This area also oversees New Century Lexington, a community-wide strategic planning effort, and the new Livability Index initiative. Under the marketing arm is membership and communications, which are geared to creating and informing members of Chamber-sponsored events, seminars, networking

sessions, and other business opportunities. The public affairs and education staff follows state and local legislation that may affect Lexington's economy and quality of life and makes recommendations for advocacy for or against such legislation. This staff also follows local issues regarding education and offers business advice to local educators like the board of education and the University of Kentucky.

Becoming a member of the Greater Lexington Chamber of Commerce is beneficial in countless ways. Business networking programs like Business Link, new member receptions, and Interview Bluegrass perpetuate business opportunities for participants. Members are kept up-to-date on issues facing the business community through the chamber's Eggs & Issues program. Young professionals are molded to become future community leaders through the Leadership Lexington and Leadership Central Kentucky programs. Small businesses can participate in an annual small business trade show and be nominated for the "Small Business of the Year." The Chamber researches economic data and publishes a number of helpful business resources such as an annual membership directory, a monthly newsletter, and assists with a minority business directory. Advertising opportunities are offered through these publications as well. The Chamber's ambassador program puts volunteers face-to-face with potential customers or business partners.

Members exhibit and network at a popular Business Link event. PHOTO BY DAVID COYLE

The Chamber's commitment to assisting minority-owned and managed businesses to thrive and prosper has been an area of concentration in recent years. In 1999, $350,000 was raised for a new five-year minority business development program. This enabled the Chamber to hire a director of minority business development, a position dedicated to the minority business development program. Since then, the number of minority-owned and managed businesses that are Chamber members has tripled. A "Minority Business of the Year" awards program has been established which annually recognizes one exceptional minority business that has prospered in Lexington's business community. The Chamber hopes to develop more programs that will help entrepreneurial minority members begin new businesses and enjoy success thereafter.

In this age of technology-driven businesses, more and more individuals are beginning companies right out of their own homes. Recognizing this trend, the Chamber developed a home-based business program to cater to those outside the corporate office. The Chamber's state-of-the-art website invites businesses to become members with the click of a mouse and offers on-line event registration, an on-line store for guests and members, job posting opportunities, mailing lists, and other Chamber and business information. The goal is to become an "e-Chamber," making all of the Chamber's resources and information available over the Internet.

As Lexington continues to grow and more businesses locate in the area, the need to think and act regionally grows increasingly important. That is why the Chamber developed a regional initiative with nine surrounding counties. This initiative is geared to help manage the growth that faces the area each year. From this effort, the Bluegrass Partnership Initiative (BPI) was formed, including two to three private sector leaders from each of these counties. Areas that are jointly affected by growth come together to discuss and recommend ways that they can work

W. T. Young Library on the University of Kentucky campus. Established 1998. PHOTO BY DAVID COYLE

together to manage it. The Lexington Chamber's board of directors includes an ex-officio member of the BPI. Quarterly regional business networking events have resulted from this effort and more cooperative programs lie ahead.

In light of becoming more regional in scope, in 2000, the Chamber began a new leadership program called Leadership Central Kentucky. This program is a spin-off from the popular Leadership Lexington program and participants learn about issues facing Central Kentucky as a whole.

As Lexington's business environment and community landscape continues to change, the Greater Lexington Chamber of Commerce will strive to remain an example to businesses through a leading-edge approach to technology, a regional approach to growth, and an empathetic approach to member services. And through partnerships with educators, government, and businesses, the Chamber will continue its quest for positive change agents in the Lexington community. •

Offices of the Greater Lexington Chamber of Commerce at Rose and Main Street. PHOTO BY DAVID COYLE

CUTTER HOMES

After 21 years in the homebuilding business, Don Cutter, owner of Cutter Homes in Lexington, decided it was time for a change. He began searching for a buyer for his reputable homebuilding company. Cutter had worked very hard to establish his business as one of the leaders in Lexington, so not any buyer would do.

Cutter Homes community entrance for a multi-year development in Scott County. PHOTO BY DAVID COYLE

Crossmann Communities, Inc. of Indianapolis became a contender after Cutter studied its record, toured its subdivisions, and spoke to industry leaders about the company. Impressed with the similarities between its operations and attitudes toward business, Cutter decided that Crossmann would be the best fit. After becoming publicly owned in the early 1990s, Crossmann was embarking on major expansion efforts and had already entered the Louisville market when Cutter approached them about buying his business. Crossmann reciprocated the interest and, in June of 1997, Cutter Homes became a wholly-owned subsidiary of Crossmann Communities, Inc.

Consistently ranked among the top 20 home-builders in the nation by *Builder Magazine*, Crossmann has maintained Cutter's strong reputation in the Central Kentucky market. They kept the "Cutter Homes" name and continue to specialize in building quality homes for first-time buyers at an affordable price. Locally, the company employs 23 people and builds over 200 homes each year.

Today, Cutter Homes represents quality, value, and service. The company holds closely the belief that a home should last a lifetime—it should reside in the best location and should be made with the highest quality materials, using skilled craftsmen.

Understanding that a good design reflects an owner's good taste, Cutter has literally hundreds of home options from which to choose. A selection center is located in the company's main office where customers can choose all of their home accessories, reducing the typical time and inconvenience it takes to make such selections.

For homeowners anxious to move in, the typical turnaround time to build a Cutter Home is 120 days, assuming no major issues arise. Contrary to what many people believe, building a home quickly does not necessarily compromise quality. In fact, because much of the building materials are pre-manufactured, there is more control over the production process. Pre-assembled building products are produced under controlled conditions in a factory setting, not on a jobsite, allowing manufacturers to use only pre-inspected materials and to maintain the highest quality required by Cutter. Advanced scheduling methods ensure that all materials arrive on the jobsite when needed and are not exposed to harsh weather for prolonged periods of time. These methods also ensure that there are always craftsmen working on the site, eliminating much downtime and controlling labor costs.

Although many of its single-family homes in Lexington seem similar to its competitors' designs, Cutter prides itself on letting buyers choose the amenities they need in their new home. This method permits the buyer to decide how they want

Completed portion of a Cutter Homes community featuring a variety of mid-sized family homes. PHOTO BY DAVID COYLE

to spend their money in designing a home that reflects personal taste and lifestyle demands. A few of the amenities the buyer selects are: appliances, type of flooring, variety of wood species, and color of cabinets and kitchen design desired. In addition, Cutter Homes offers cutting-edge features and options such as premium cable for high-speed Internet connectivity throughout the home, security prewires, home office technology, and home theatre sound systems.

Special financing options set Cutter Homes apart from other homebuilders. Recognizing that most of its customers are middle-income families, Cutter offers a number of flexible programs to finance a new home. For example, the Buy & Save Plan is similar to "layaway," giving the customer up to six months to save the down payment for a new home. If already a homeowner, Cutter will offer to buy the existing home at an agreed upon value should the homeowner be unable to sell by the time their new Cutter home is ready. If a prospective buyer is approved for an FHA loan, they may also qualify for a gift of three percent of the sale price from the nonprofit organization, Nehemiah. Whatever the circumstance, Cutter works with a variety of lending organizations to provide the best available financing programs, helping customers achieve the "American Dream" of owning a new home.

The importance of providing exceptional customer service before and after the sale is evident through Cutter Homes' quality assurance team. This team monitors customer satisfaction through mail surveys and personal phone calls, giving customers the opportunity to provide constructive feedback on the service they received. This feedback keeps Cutter informed about customers' needs, likes, and dislikes, and helps improve customer service year after year.

Cutter Homes is active in community service activities in an attempt to return a portion of their success to the community. The company participates in building Habitat for Humanity homes for families that otherwise may never be able to own a home. The staff participates in the United Way employee-giving program that continues to grow each year. A future goal for Cutter Homes is to become more involved in youth programs

An open kitchen and family room floor plan is one of the many designs Cutter Homes offers for today's family lifestyle. PHOTO BY DAVID COYLE

and education. Currently, for every house that is closed by Cutter, a certain number of dollars is contributed to an educational program.

The management and staff also maintain involvement in local professional organizations such as the Home Builders Association of Lexington. In 1996, Don Cutter was named "Home Builder of the Year" by the Lexington association. Each year, Cutter Homes are featured in the Association's Grand Tour of Homes, during which Cutter has received innumerable awards for best floorplans and merchandising.

Cutter homes hopes to expand to properties on all sides of the city in the coming years. The company plans to develop more of its own property and focus on high volume, yet high quality subdivisions. Most importantly, Cutter Homes will continue the legacy that Don Cutter left behind and will serve the Lexington and Central Kentucky market with quality, service, and value.

For more information on Cutter Homes or Crossmann Communities, visit their Web sites at www.cutterhomesltd.com, or www.croscom.com. •

A Cutter home during the framing stage of construction. PHOTO BY DAVID COYLE

WKYT-TV

*O*n September 30, 1957, WKYT-TV went on the air in Central Kentucky as a CBS affiliate with a staff of about 15, broadcasting from a small building in eastern Fayette County.

WKYT-TV, 2851 Winchester Road, Lexington, Kentucky. PHOTO BY STEWART BOWMAN

In 1967, WKYT-TV was sold to Garvice Kincaid's Kentucky Central Life Insurance Company. A Lexington entrepreneur, Kincaid had a vision. Already the owner of several banks, a life insurance company, a conglomerate of radio stations, and a few orange groves in Florida, Kincaid sought to diversify his business interests even further. To accommodate growth, a new facility was built in 1968 and is still home to WKYT-TV today. Now, approximately 130 employees are responsible for the daily operations of the station.

Kincaid hired Ralph Gabbard in 1972, as sales manager, and soon promoted him to general manager. Under Gabbard's leadership, WKYT-TV became what is today the most watched television station in the market. He made the University of Kentucky Sports franchise an important element, but local news was clearly the dominant theme. At presstime, WKYT-TV's DMA ranking was 66th in the country, broadcasting to over 400,000 households in Central and Eastern Kentucky.

Gabbard recognized that many Eastern Kentucky counties were receiving their television signals from Tennessee and West Virginia. He convinced Kentucky Central TV, Inc. to build WYMT (We're Your Mountain Television) in 1985. Shortly thereafter, he hired Wayne Martin to lead the sales effort and he later became the station's general manager. Former U.S. Senator Wendell Ford called WYMT "the best thing to happen to Eastern Kentucky since roads."

Kentucky Central TV (WKYT and WYMT) with news bureaus now in Pikeville and Middlesboro,

along with Frankfort, television stations in Hazard and Lexington, was providing more local news and information coverage to Kentuckians than any other television source.

In 1994, Gray Communications, based in Atlanta, Georgia, purchased Kentucky Central TV. Gabbard was named president of the Gray broadcast group and Martin president of WKYT and WYMT. Under Gray and CEO J. Mack Robinson, there was a continued commitment to localism and public service. Gray Kentucky TV takes great pride in the quality and quantity of service to Central and Eastern Kentuckians, provided by their talented employees. These employees are committed to serving the public interest, contributing to the communities they serve, and increasing shareholder value.

Today, WKYT-TV still upholds the standards established by Garvice Kincaid, nurtured by Ralph Gabbard, and sustained by Wayne Martin and the current WKYT staff. These standards are reflected in the station's mission statement: "WKYT-TV will be a community leader, through the operation of a commercial television station in the public interest, by informing and entertaining our viewers with high quality local news and entertainment programming while providing services to help our clients achieve financial prosperity." •

Left to Right: Rob Bromley, Sam Dick, Barbara Bailey, and Brian Collins. 27 Newsfirst's 6 P.M. anchor team. PHOTO BY STEWART BOWMAN

THE MASON & HANGER GROUP

a Day & Zimmermann company

It was in 1827 when Claiborne Rice Mason began his career and founded his company in Alexandria, Virginia. With a mule, cart, pick, and shovel, Mason completed a small dirt-moving contract for a road construction project. Before he knew it, Mason was helping the state of Virginia develop its railroads and this effort eventually led his growing company to Kentucky.

21st Century Instruction Center—300,000 square feet.

The company's first project in Kentucky was the construction of a section of track in northern Kentucky in 1875. Other rail work in Kentucky followed and in 1881, Kentucky became the home of Mason & Hanger.

Over the next hundred years or so, Mason's company would help to change the face of America with involvement in such landmark public-works projects as: the Grand Coulee and Merriman dams; the New York City subway tunnels; the George Washington Bridge foundations; the Lincoln, Brooklyn Battery, and Boston Harbor tunnels; and the Ray Hill Tunnel on the Pennsylvania Turnpike.

21st Century Instruction Center three-story entry atrium.

In 1999, The Mason & Hanger Group merged with Day & Zimmermann of Philadelphia, a company with similar histories and corporate values. This merger produced a company with an impressive 250 years of combined experience in architecture, engineering, and construction.

Headquartered in Lexington, The Mason & Hanger Group continues its legacy as the oldest, continuously operated engineering and construction firm in the United States. It is the 10th oldest firm in Kentucky and

has contributed to some of the area's most recognizable landmarks. Mason & Hanger is one of a small sampling of companies in Kentucky with architecture, engineering and construction capabilities, and has one of the largest architectural staffs in the state.

The group's 100-plus employees—based in Lexington and Louisville, Kentucky—provide architectural, engineering, and construction services to clients locally, regionally, and nationally. A major part of the company's business is in providing architectural and engineering design services for the nation's military and federal agencies. Other clients include many of America's major corporations, as well as local and state government agencies.

The company makes a concerted effort to share its expertise with the local community. Mason & Hanger has been involved in the development of local landmarks including the Lexington-Fayette Urban County Government building, Blue Grass Airport, Rupp Arena and the Civic Center complex, and downtown's scenic Thoroughbred Park.

Looking to the future, Mason & Hanger will continue to change to meet the demands of an ever-changing industry while maintaining its core values of safety, quality, and integrity. Mason & Hanger will continue to structure its business practices according to its customers' needs, streamline processes for improved efficiency, and provide "total package" architecture, engineering, and construction services to its clients. •

Grand Coulee Dam.

HENKEL-DENMARK

*K*nown *for its scenic beauty, it is no secret that the city of Lexington and the surrounding bluegrass country is a special place. Although much of the rural countryside is natural, the bluegrass area is best known for its miles of impeccably manicured horse farms. It seems the city's suburban residents and corporate citizens also uphold the tradition of beautiful landscaping.*

The Partnership, Gordon Denmark and Bill Henkel. PHOTO BY DAVID COYLE

It is companies like Henkel-Denmark that not only create Lexington's beautiful landscapes, but maintain them as well. When a company has over 46 years of combined experience in the landscape design and maintenance, it learns a few things along the way. And, when this company is the landscape design and maintenance firm of Henkel-Denmark, that experience is utilized to create beautiful, award-winning gardens and landscapes that make an impression, even in an area that takes its gardens as seriously as Lexington does.

Henkel-Denmark believes that planning is essential for effective landscaping, from the smallest garden to the largest landscaping project. The company's designers pride themselves on seeing the "big picture," which enables them to plan effectively and execute award-winning designs. From planning and construction—including lighting and masonry—to implementation and maintenance, Henkel-Denmark does it all.

And like all great art, creating award-winning landscapes only looks easy. Behind the scenes, it's a group effort from all of Henkel-Denmark's landscaping professionals. Maintenance and landscape foremen, installers, maintainers, and other laborers make up the company's landscaping team roster.

Henkel-Denmark's landscaping and maintenance teams serve both residential and commercial markets. On the commercial maintenance side of things, the company services hospitals, apartment complexes, office buildings, office parks, commercial sites, and shopping centers. For residential and commercial landscaping clients, Henkel-Denmark designs and installs perennial and annual gardens, herb gardens, pools, patios, terraces, and decks.

What sets Henkel-Denmark apart from the many landscaping businesses in the area is the ability to provide both landscape design and building services to its clients. It is by offering this "total package" to clients, combined with efficiency and impeccable customer service that the company has realized such great success.

With a long and varied list featuring prominent horse farms, apartment communities, office complexes, and hospitals, as well as private homes, Henkel-Denmark draws on a vast wealth of experience and talent in all types of landscaping.

Henkel-Denmark stays on the cutting-edge of the landscaping industry through its involvement in professional organizations such as the Associated Landscape Contractors of America, the American Society of Landscape Architects, Central Kentucky Ornamental & Turf Association, and the Kentucky Nurserymen's Association. As a community service, the company provides landscaping and planting for downtown parks and community non-profit organizations.

Henkel-Denmark takes great pride in the beautiful gardens and landscapes it creates and manages. The company plans to ensure that businesses, families, and individuals throughout Lexington will continue to enjoy them for many years to come. •

Seasonal garden color at The Racquet Club Apartments. PHOTO BY DAVID COYLE

HOLMAN PLUMBING, HEATING & AIR CONDITIONING

In 1970, Jim Holman was a young man, just out of high school. The Vietnam War was underway, and young men throughout the country were being called to serve—Holman would be one of them. During bootcamp, an illness quickly sent Holman back home to Lexington. A friend of Holman's was working for a reputable plumbing company and recruited him for an apprenticeship there. Little did he realize that this would be the beginning of a life-long career.

Within 18 months, Holman earned his "Journeyman's license," which would allow him to physically administer plumbing services. In 1972, he earned his Master's license, providing the opportunity to start a business of his own. With a truck and his newfound set of skills, he began Holman Plumbing that year.

Early on, the focus of Holman Plumbing was on service work. Holman himself would service existing plumbing systems in commercial and residential properties throughout Lexington. As demand grew and Holman's reputation spread, he hired employees to help service his growing customer base. All the while, Holman also served as a Lexington firefighter. Firefighting would eventually lead to an injury that would prevent him from being able to do the physical labor required by the plumbing business. He was forced into the office and became dependent on others to service Holman Plumbing's customers. It was then that Holman began to focus on recruiting and retaining quality employees for his business.

As the company grew, the opportunity to diversify came along. Heating and air conditioning installation, maintenance, and repair became a complementary business to plumbing. Holman took advantage of this opportunity, hiring and training employees for this type of work. Holman Plumbing eventually became Holman Plumbing, Heating & Air Conditioning.

Some 60 employees now service Holman's large customer base, primarily consisting of commercial properties throughout

The beginning.

The present. PHOTO BY DAVID COYLE

Lexington and Central Kentucky. Holman's work not only consists of maintenance on existing systems, but also on commercial construction, design/build, and installation of plumbing, heating and air conditioning systems. Holman prides itself on the ability to provide custom plumbing, heating and air conditioning solutions on a reasonable budget.

Holman attributes much of the company's success to hiring and retaining quality employees. Several of Holman's service technicians have over 25 years experience in commercial plumbing, heating and air conditioning, a rarity in this line of work. Holman helps employees grow with the company by offering a profit-sharing program. The company's commitment to retaining quality employees is demonstrated by the fact that no employee in Holman's history has ever been laid off for lack of work. When the company experiences "down time" due to poor weather or a slow economy, employees are cross-trained and help one another learn new techniques and tricks of the trade.

So no matter how large Holman Plumbing, Heating & Air Conditioning becomes, the company will always hold steadfast to the idea that "you're only as good as your employees." The company intends to continue its long-lasting tradition of providing custom plumbing, heating, and air conditioning solutions to its customers for years to come. •

LEXINGTON HERALD-LEADER

exington and much of Kentucky look daily to the Lexington Herald-Leader *for insights and information. The newspaper covers everything from courthouse to statehouse, from box scores to box office with a rapidity that John Bradford never envisioned.*

It was Bradford who, in 1785, responded to Lexingtonians' urgent pleas for a newspaper by procuring a second-hand printing press from Philadelphia. He set up shop at the corner of present-day Main and Broadway and printed the premier issue of the *Kentucky Gazette*—the first newspaper "west of the Alleghenies"—on August 11, 1787. From concept to copy, the project took two years.

Two centuries later, *the Lexington Herald-Leader*, descendant of Bradford's *Kentucky Gazette*, has developed into the definitive news source not only for Lexington, but for all of Central and Eastern Kentucky, says Pam Luecke, editor and senior vice president. "Most of our news is gathered in Lexington, but we maintain eight bureaus and circulate in 76 counties—nearly two-thirds of the state," she says. "We deploy our reporters in areas where they can find stories that are important to the people of Kentucky."

In addition to delivering news, the Herald-Leader serves as a public forum. "We give people a voice to express their opinions about state and community issues, and we attempt to provide leadership on those issues," says Tim Kelly, president and publisher.

On its editorial and opinions pages, the newspaper offers a frank exchange of views—including its own—according to Vanessa Gallman, editorial page editor. "When we write editorials,

Central and Eastern Kentucky's primary source of news and information.

we are analytical, provocative, and educational about the issues, but it's not the gospel," she says. "Ours is just one take on an issue of the day."

And the newspaper's partnership with the community is not limited to words. "We try to be a leading corporate citizen by supporting community projects and programs and through our association with the John S. and James L. Knight Foundation," says Kelly.

In fact, during the past decade, the foundation has given more than $12 million to Kentucky projects, institutions, and agencies. The *Herald-Leader* also contributes to more than 100 groups and every year gives away more than a half-million dollars' worth of advertising space to help qualified organizations promote special events and fund-raisers.

The *Herald-Leader*, says Kelly, is known nationally for "playing above its head." Since 1986, the newspaper has been awarded journalism's highest honor, the Pulitzer Prize, three times—for investigative reporting, editorial writing, and editorial cartooning. The *Herald-Leader* has also been recognized every year since 1981 for having one of the nation's 10 best sports sections; its religion section won two national awards in 2000.

While readers rely on the *Herald-Leader* for information, businesses bank on the newspaper's ability to deliver their message throughout the market, says Ann Caulkins, senior vice president for sales and marketing. "If an advertiser wants to reach the most people, the *Herald-Leader* is far and away the most efficient vehicle," she says. On an average day, more than 400,000 Kentuckians read the Lexington newspaper.

Delivering the region's primary news source is faster and more comprehensive than in Bradford's day, but not simpler, says Luecke. "We manufacture a new product every day—we write, edit, illustrate, print and package it," she says. "We're only half-kidding when we call it 'The Daily Miracle.'" •

The Equine Industry

MILL RIDGE FARM

*H*er roots in the horse industry are as deep as they come. Alice Chandler's great grandfather began a family legacy in horse farming that would last for over a century.

Sunrise at Mill Ridge. PHOTO BY STEWART BOWMAN

Chandler, owner of Lexington's Mill Ridge Farm, grew up entrenched in the breeding, training, racing, and selling of Thoroughbred horses. Her father was Hal Price Headley, a revered owner, breeder, and trainer of Thoroughbreds and the man credited with building Keeneland Race Course, one of the nation's most historic and renowned Thoroughbred racing facilities. Headley owned 2,016 acres of lush Bluegrass countryside, known as Beaumont Farm. Recognizing that breeding horses alone could not always pay the bills, Headley also grew tobacco and raised cattle on Beaumont to ensure the farm could be self-sufficient.

As a young girl, Chandler began learning the horse farming business from her father. As with most young girls, she fell in love with the majestic giants and admired her father for the hard work and dedication he put into his business.

Headley was not your typical horseman who bought and sold horses and let others worry about their care. He expected a lot from his employees but never expected them to do anything he wouldn't do himself. Headley was especially interested in developing ways to care for a

Mill Ridge racing colors. PHOTO BY STEWART BOWMAN

horse's feet, teaching his employees how to properly shoe horses to decrease the likelihood of discomfort and injury. He raced mostly his own horses and, once their racing days ended, Headley returned them to Beaumont.

In 1933, Lexington's only Thoroughbred racetrack closed, leaving horse owners and trainers desperate for a convenient racing facility. Headley had a vision for a new facility that would bring people together to celebrate the horse. Attracting bettors was secondary to this vision. In 1936, through the leadership of Headley, Keeneland Race Course opened to horsemen, horse admirers, and the mildly curious. In line with Headley's vision, Keeneland was inviting to people of all walks of life. Its purpose was to share in the entertainment of the sport and the betterment of the horse.

Headley always struggled with whether or not to race his own horses at Keeneland. He received criticism if he did, and even more if he didn't.

Nevertheless, his champions won a number of races at Keeneland, including several stakes races. Tragically, yet somewhat appropriately, Headley suffered a heart attack and died at his beloved Keeneland during an early morning workout session.

In 1962, after the death of her father, Chandler was inspired to continue her father's legacy. She turned 286 acres of what was once Beaumont Farm into Mill Ridge Farm. Mill Ridge was home to only four mares and, to make ends meet, Chandler began boarding horses for friends and family. Four employees tended the farm, one of whom still works there today. Mill Ridge now boasts 1,050 acres.

Only two years after Mill Ridge opened for business, one of the farm's original broodmares bore a champion colt. Her father, who told her that someday the mare may "throw you a racehorse," gave the broodmare, Attica, to Chandler. In 1966, Chandler sold the colt who would be Sir Ivor to Raymond Guest, the Ambassador to Ireland at Keeneland's Thoroughbred horse sales. This athletic Thoroughbred eventually became the champion two-year-old in England and the champion three-year-old in Europe. The sale of Sir Ivor changed the face of Keeneland's Thoroughbred horse sales, attracting more and more international buyers from across the globe.

A "Thorough-general" farm, as Chandler calls it, Mill Ridge is now home to approximately 200 mares and six stallions. Foals are either sold at auction or are kept to eventually race under the farm's silks or for clients.

Mill Ridge Farm has come far from its somewhat humble beginnings. It is now one of the leading consignors of Thoroughbred horses in the nation. In 1999, *Thoroughbred Times* named Mill Ridge Farm as the sixth top consignor, grossing Thoroughbred sales of $20.7 million. In September of that year,

Through the sycamore trees. PHOTO BY STEWART BOWMAN

Retired broodmares. PHOTO BY DAVID COYLE

Mill Ridge sold a colt for a stunning $2.25 million, a filly for $1.1 million, and another filly for $650,000.

Mill Ridge has produced 10 stakes winners: Sir Ivor, Keeper Hill, Nicosia, Ciao, Hadif, Secret Hello, Flemensfirth, Golden Gear, Rash Statement, and Pillow Talk. The farm's enormous success is attributed to a superior staff, which now numbers close to 60, and to being selective about to whom and by whom the farm's horses are bred. Since day one, Chandler has held a strict policy of only doing business with her trusted friends. She professes that this has been key to her ability to compete as one of the leading Thoroughbred owners and breeders in the world.

The stallions that stand at stud at Mill Ridge can also be credited with the farm's success. Diesis is a world-class sire responsible for producing some of the best young champions in the world. At presstime, Diesis had sired 62 stakes winners and is a well-respected broodmare sire with 21 stakes winners produced by his daughters. He was also the sire of three English Oaks winners. Gone West is considered by

many to be the heir apparent to his legendary sire Mr. Prospector, a stallion who, before his death in 1999, produced a remarkable number of champion Thoroughbreds. Gone West's offspring are continually proving their worth. Nearly one in four starters from Gone West becomes a stakes horse. His yearlings are sought after in yearling auctions due to class, soundness, and versatility.

Throughout Chandler's career, she has been actively involved in associations charged with the betterment of horse racing. She has been a member of the Kentucky Thoroughbred Owners and Breeders Association since 1976 and served as secretary, treasurer, vice president, and president. In 1999, she was appointed chair of the Gluck Equine Research Center, an organization dedicated to medical research for the equine industry. In 2000, Chandler was appointed by Governor Paul Patton to the Kentucky Racing Commission and the Equine Drug Council. She is one of the founding members of S.O.I.L., an acronym for "Save Our Irreplaceable Land." This organization was formed to prevent unnecessary airport expansion from destroying Central Kentucky's rich Bluegrass countryside.

Friendly yearlings. PHOTO BY STEWART BOWMAN

And Chandler isn't only admired by those in her industry, the community recognizes her and her family's contributions to the area. In 2000, Chandler was honored by the Lexington Chapter of National Association of Women Business Owners with their 2000 Winner's Circle Award. The award is given each year to the

Curiosity. PHOTO BY STEWART BOWMAN

woman who has shown "outstanding leadership, financial stamina and control, participated in the community, and is dedicated to furthering other women in business." Chandler is respected as one of the first women to overcome stereotypes of women horse owners and breeders and to position herself as a leader in that industry.

The group that Chandler believes will be important to the future of horse racing is the National Thoroughbred Racing Association. The NTRA is working to develop strict racing policies that will provide a unified front for the industry.

Chandler attributes the success of Mill Ridge Farm to her land, location, and team of dedicated horsemen. Being near Blue Grass Airport and Keeneland has contributed to the farm's accessibility. She considers her farm managers to be the best in the business.

A strong economy is key to Mill Ridge Farm's future success. In a strong economy, racing purses increase and attract more buyers, sellers, and bettors to the sport. Chandler believes that Lexington's horse industry will continue to prosper, given the economy remains strong. Most of all, Chandler believes that

Here's looking at you! PHOTO BY DAVID COYLE

the preservation of greenspace in Lexington and the surrounding Bluegrass region will be the essential ingredient to a surviving, prosperous horse industry. •

Rolling land raises good horses. PHOTO BY STEWART BOWMAN

ROOD & RIDDLE EQUINE HOSPITAL

$\mathcal{A}$s the "Horse Capital of the World," it is no secret that Lexington is the top producer of Thoroughbred racehorses. These strong, majestic creatures are bred and trained to be champions on the racetrack. As for all athletes, it is important that these horses be in tip-top condition when facing intense competition.

The lovely landscape enhances the entrance leading to the hospital complex in the background. PHOTO BY STEWART BOWMAN

For years, full-service equine medical facilities were limited. Most equine veterinarians were ambulatory, meaning they traveled from horse farm to horse farm to treat their giant patients. Recognizing the limitations that an ambulatory practice posed, Dr. Thomas Riddle and Dr. William Rood wanted to do more to serve the nation's horse industry. Despite the fact that the industry was in a bit of slump, the doctors took a "leap of faith" and relied on their gut instincts to open the Rood & Riddle Equine Hospital in 1986. Their vision was to become the "Mayo Clinic" for the equine world.

The hospital's beginnings included the two founding and four other veterinarians, nine staff members, and a 25,000 square-foot facility. Rood & Riddle now has an international reputation for their work in orthopedics, general surgery, neonatology, and reproduction. The staff has grown to a healthy 155, 30 of which are

veterinarians, and the facility has expanded to an enormous 68,000 square feet.

Similar to what you would find at a full-service hospital built for humans, Rood & Riddle is equipped with intensive care, isolation, and neonatal units so that specialized care can be administered free from interruption. Ninety-two stalls provide enough capacity to house that many horses at once and treatment is also available on an outpatient basis. A laboratory, diagnostic imaging center, pharmacy, radiology, and surgery suites complement the hospital's full-service nature.

Rood & Riddle is now one of the largest equine hospitals in the world, treating over 7,000 horses each year and performing in excess of 3,500 surgeries. Thousands of Thoroughbred champions, including Triple Crown Winner Seattle Slew, are among those brought back to health at the hospital each year. Although Thoroughbreds comprise the hospital's primary patient load, all breeds are among the hospital's clientele including Standardbreds, Warmbloods, Quarter Horses, Saddlebreds, and Walking Horses, reflective of Kentucky's diverse horse industry.

The majority of Rood & Riddle's patients reside in Central Kentucky, but horses from all over the world are treated here. Even Queen Elizabeth II has entrusted her horses to the care of Rood & Riddle. Other famous names that have sent their champions to the hospital are country music star Reba McIntyre,

Dr. Larry Bramlage interprets radiographs of a horse's front ankle. PHOTO BY STEWART BOWMAN

The partners of the practice are (from left to right): Drs. Larry Bramlage, Rolf Embertson, Bill Rood, Tom Riddle, Scott Pierce, and Bill Bernard. PHOTO BY DAVID COYLE

accomplished actor/director Robert Duval, and late '80s rap music phenomenon MC Hammer.

The hospital's highly skilled medical staff is key to its success. Orthopedic and soft tissue surgeons, general surgeons, internal medicine specialists, ambulatory veterinarians, and lameness clinicians administer Rood & Riddle's specialized medical and surgical care. Ambulatory veterinarians provide off-site care for 40 to 50 local farms and specialize in fertility and reproduction treatment for over 3,000 broodmares. These doctors also evaluate foals for proper development and administer preventative healthcare measures.

The staff's impressive resume includes Board certifications in surgery, internal medicine, cardiology, and ophthalmology. Staff members are involved in a long list of equine-related associations such as the American Association of Equine Practitioners, the Thoroughbred Owners and Breeders Association, and the National Thoroughbred Racing Association, to name a few. Several Rood & Riddle veterinarians are well-published and are frequently asked to speak nationally and internationally on issues facing the industry. Employees are involved in a number of community service and civic activities including blood drives, fundraisers that benefit Multiple Sclerosis programs, Central Kentucky Riding for the Handicapped, and a number of area horse shows and events.

Rood & Riddle is not a teaching hospital, but it does offer hands-on learning opportunities through internship and externship programs.

Interns rotate through surgery, medicine, and anesthesia services and receive a level of post-graduate training that allows them to pursue a residency program. Veterinary students from all over the world can complete their externship requirement with Rood & Riddle, an intense two- to four-week program. On-site housing is available for four students at a time, although additional students are accepted if they are housed off-site. Externs work with each surgeon on a rotational basis, and may opt to ride with ambulatory doctors in the rotation. Externs may also observe equine specialists in cardiology, acupuncture, lameness examination, reproduction, internal medicine, neonatology, orthopedic and soft tissue surgery, and radiology.

Drawing on human medicine, treatment for creatures of the equine persuasion has become increasingly advanced over Rood & Riddle's 15-year existence. The introduction of the arthroscope has enabled veterinarians to return horses to their championship form after surgery. Horses are flown in from all over the world for the best orthopedic surgery available today. Huge advances in neonatal intensive care have ensured that at-risk foals can grow up to become prize-winning horses.

Quality in veterinary care is a tradition at Rood & Riddle Equine Hospital. As medical and surgical techniques become more advanced, the hospital's team of highly skilled medical staff will continue to learn and apply their knowledge to improving the quality of care for the equine industry. •

A horse undergoes arthroscopic surgery. PHOTO BY STEWART BOWMAN

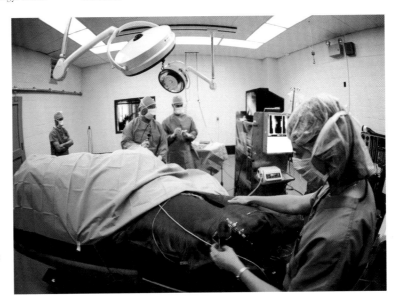

COBRA FARM

*A*t an early age, Gary Biszantz developed a deep passion for Thoroughbred horse racing. Having grown up in California, he attended Thoroughbred races with his father, a horseman himself, at the world-renowned racetrack of Santa Anita. In 1956, Biszantz took his passion a step further when he purchased his first Thoroughbred horse, Affirm Miss.

That same year, Affirm Miss brought home a win for Biszantz at Santa Anita, only fueling his love and desire for success in the sport.

After attending sales and races in Kentucky for years, it was Biszantz's dream to own a farm in the Bluegrass. In 1995, he purchased an 80-acre farm on the north side of Fayette County. It was not only its impeccably manicured grounds and paddocks, but its impressive history as the birthplace of the 1977 Triple Crown Winner Seattle Slew and 1993 Two-Year-Old Champion Colt Dehere, which drew him to this particular farm. Biszantz renamed the farm "Cobra Farm" after his successful Cobra Golf company. He retained farm managers Mike Owens and Jeanne Cox-Owens. Jeanne was named "Kentucky Thoroughbred Farm Manager of the Year" in 1998, an award given annually for contributions to both the equine industry and community outreach.

In 1999, Biszantz purchased 145 acres of adjoining land, increasing Cobra Farm's acreage to 225. The farm now features six barns with 84 stalls and employs about 20 people including grooms, maintenance and landscaping personnel, and an administrative staff.

Main foaling barn, birthplace of Seattle Slew.

Cobra Farm is a broodmare and yearling operation, home to more than two dozen top-quality broodmares, their weanlings and yearlings. The farm keeps mares to produce offspring to race under the Cobra Farm green and gold silks. Because it is a private farm, Cobra staff members are able to spend a significant amount of time nurturing and caring for the farm's yearly crop of foals. They get accustomed to human contact but are kept outdoors in their natural environment most all of the time.

Since 1992 and through the end of 2000, horses owned by Biszantz (some owned in partnership) have made more than 1,500 race starts with over 280 wins and finishing "in the money" 51 percent of the time. Not only has Cobra Farm been successful with such graded stakes winners as Old Trieste, Cobra King and Savinio in this country, it has won prestigious races in Argentina with Grade 1 winners Venusberg and La Galerie. The farm boasts Lord Grillo , the only three-year-old colt to win Grade 1 races in both hemispheres in the same year. Cobra Farm has also campaigned runners in France where Splendid Senor won the Prix de la Place Vendome in 1998.

Biszantz credits his success to a philosophy woven around quality and winning, by believing that you must first have the product, give the horse a chance to show its ability, and run it where it has the best opportunity for success. However, financial gain isn't what Biszantz and his Cobra Farm staff believe is the most important part of the sport. It's to achieve the goals of a great horse—to win the classics, the great races.

Protecting Lexington's rich farmland is high priority for Biszantz and the Cobra Farm staff. As development threatens Lexington's rural landscape, the farm advocates for the preservation of the area's agricultural land. At presstime, the horse industry is Kentucky's number one agricultural industry. It has created and supported hundreds of auxiliary businesses, not only in Kentucky, but throughout the world. The industry employs hundreds upon thousands of

Owners, Gary and Betty Biszantz, at entrance to Cobra Farm.

people, providing a living to families from the United States, to Europe, to the Middle East.

Improving the horse industry is also a focus for Cobra Farm. That is why Biszantz, as well as several of Cobra's staff members, are involved in a number of industry organizations and associations geared to doing just that. Biszantz has served on the Executive Committee and the Graded Stakes Committee of the Thoroughbred Owners and Breeders Association, as well as the board of directors for the Breeder's Cup. In 1999, Biszantz was elected into membership of the prestigious Jockey Club. He was also instrumental in the formation of the National Thoroughbred Association, the forerunner of the present-day National Thoroughbred Racing Association. Farm managers Jeanne Cox-Owens and Mike Owens are actively involved in the Kentucky Thoroughbred Farm Managers Club, ReRun, Inc., and Central Kentucky Racing for the Handicapped, a therapeutic riding program.

Biszantz is very active in philanthropy through his Biszantz Charitable Foundation, which places special emphasis on children's activities. Organizations like the YMCA and the Idaho Youth Ranch benefit from Biszantz's foundation. Through the foundation, Biszantz purchased a farm for the United Pegasus Foundation that retrains, rescues, and gives homes to retired racehorses and rehabilitates injured horses. The foundation supports California Equine Retirement Foundation, a ranch for retired racehorses. It is supportive of the Athletic Performance Laboratory, the Center for Equine Health, the Piedra

Cobra Farm Silks.

Foundation, the Helen Woodward Animal Hospital, the Grayson-Jockey Club Research Foundation, and the Don MacBeth Jockey Fund. In March of 1999, the Association of Racing Commissioners International awarded Biszantz their annual "Animal Welfare" award. In April of the same year, the Kentucky Thoroughbred Owners and Breeders Association awarded him "Humanitarian of the Year".

The new millennium brings new challenges for Cobra Farm and the Thoroughbred horse industry. No matter what challenges Biszantz and his staff may face in the future, one goal will remain constant: to continually breed and produce top-class, stakes winning Thoroughbreds and uphold the strong tradition of Cobra Farm. •

Mike and Jeanne Owens with stakes winning Star of Goshen and her 2000 A.P. Indy Colt.

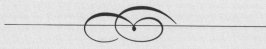

Health Care

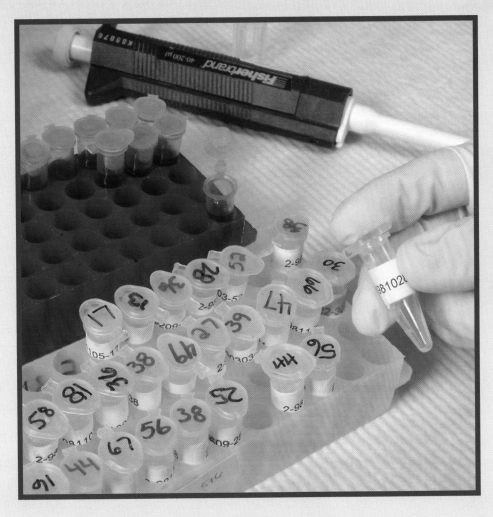

KENTUCKY EAR, NOSE & THROAT

he physicians of Kentucky Ear, Nose & Throat are head and neck surgeons who specialize in the treatment of ear, nose, and throat disease for patients of all ages. The clinic focuses on caring for patients with problems such as ear infections, sinus infections, tumors in the head and neck region, voice disorders, and hearing loss. The physicians of Kentucky Ear, Nose & Throat perform sinus, nasal, and throat surgery, implant ear tubes in children, treat head and neck cancer, and remove tonsils.

Administrator Sherry King discusses the clinic flow with Peggy Dishman. PHOTO BY STEWART BOWMAN

The practice continued to grow as more and more patients began learning about Kentucky Ear, Nose & Throat's broad range of care. Dr. Kenneth "Tad" Hughes, also a graduate of the Mayo Clinic Residency Program, was the next surgeon to join the group. Dr. Hughes brought his interest in pediatric otolaryngological problems and established a voice clinic in the practice.

At that time, Kentucky Ear, Nose & Throat employed more than 25 people including three original board-certified physicians, a nurse practitioner, and four audiologists. Due to high patient volume, the medical staff expanded again to include Dr. Alberto Laureano, a surgeon and graduate of Southern Illinois University. Also board-certified, he brought an interest in allergy diagnosis and treatment as well as unique approaches to sinus disease.

Dr. Osetinsky reviews a patient chart before surgery. PHOTO BY STEWART BOWMAN

The practice began through the vision of Dr. Keith Alexander after completing his residency at the Ohio State University in 1990. Board-certified in Otolaryngology and trained as a head and neck surgeon, Dr. Alexander knew he could combine both his medical and his surgical skills to create a complete, full-service ear, nose, and throat care center. He began Kentucky Ear, Nose & Throat with two support staff members and an audiologist in a 1,800-square-foot facility at Central Baptist Hospital that same year.

When the community began to grow and the referral volume increased, Dr. Greg Osetinsky joined the practice. Dr. Osetinsky was a faculty member at the University of Kentucky at that time and received his training at the Mayo Clinic. Also board-certified in Otolaryngology, he brought an interest in tumors in the head and neck region.

The facility at Central Baptist Hospital has expanded twice since opening in 1990—first to 6,000 square feet and again to 10,000 square feet. Kentucky Ear, Nose & Throat has satellite offices in other Central Kentucky counties including Franklin and Madison County. Over 20,000 patients visit the clinic each year and over 1,000 physicians have referred patients to the practice.

Through continuing education programs and involvement in professional associations, the physicians and staff at Kentucky Ear, Nose & Throat stay up-to-date on the latest in research, treatment, and care of ear, nose, and throat diseases. The physicians are members of such professional associations as Bluegrass Academy of Otolaryngology, Lexington Medical Society, Kentucky Medical Association, American Medical Association, the American Academy of Otolaryngology, American Academy of Otolaryngic Allergy, American Academy of Facial Plastic Surgeons, and the American College of Surgeons. All have published a variety of scientific articles on issues relating to the field. Dr. Osetinsky has served as president of the Lexington Medical Society. Dr. Hughes served as a delegate to the Kentucky Medical Association and the Lexington Medical Society. He also is on the board of Faith Pharmacy, assisting the indigent with their medications.

A well-trained medical staff is primary to administering treatment, but Kentucky Ear, Nose & Throat places great importance on having the most state-of-the-art in medical technology and equipment. A videostroboscopy helps to diagnose vocal cord abnormalities and other problems that occur in the throat. The practice has a voice clinic completely devoted to patients with vocal problems. Computer analysis of the inner ear assists the physicians in diagnosing the etiology of dizziness, imbalance, and hearing loss in patients of all ages. The practice dispenses state-of-the-art digital, conventional, and programmable hearing aids, all of which are customized by the audiologists to match sound amplification to the precise amount of hearing loss.

The nurses and administrative staff also keep current on issues relating to health care such as Medicare reform, managed care contracting, procedural coding, and customer service. Many staff members belong to organizations like the Association of Otolaryngology Administrators, Medical Group Management Association, Society of Head and Neck Nurses, and the local chapters of management and nursing.

As more and more people are affected by diseases of the ear, nose, and throat, the physicians and staff of Kentucky Ear, Nose & Throat-Head and Neck will strive to provide the most thorough and appropriate care possible. As new and different medical issues arise, Kentucky Ear, Nose & Throat will continue their dedication to learning and utilizing the most current techniques and treatments. •

Dr. Tad Hughes and Dr. Greg Osetinsky consult on a difficult patient. PHOTO BY STEWART BOWMAN

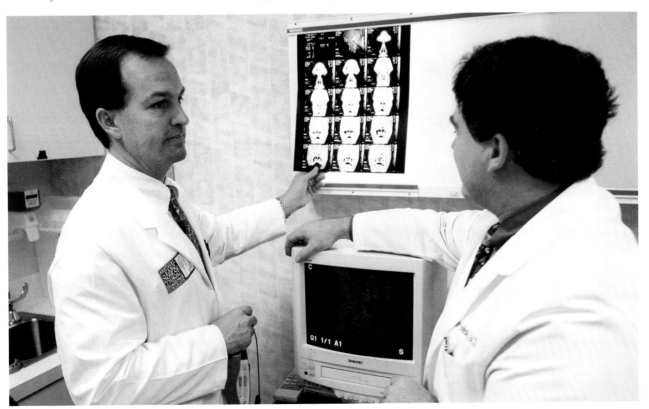

UNITED SURGICAL ASSOCIATES

What do you get when you combine three of the largest surgical groups in Central Kentucky into one? Some would say the most comprehensive, experienced surgical practice in Lexington. In 1998, three of Central Kentucky's largest surgical groups—Lexington Surgeons, Bluegrass Surgical Group, and Surgical Associates—combined to form United Surgical Associates, PSC.

The goal: to improve patient care through the collaboration of expertise and to reduce business costs by sharing administrative and support personnel.

The group of over a dozen dynamic physicians provides comprehensive coverage of general and vascular surgery at all of Lexington's major hospitals including St. Joseph Hospital, Samaritan Hospital, Central Baptist Hospital, St. Joseph East, and HealthSouth Ambulatory Surgical Center, as well as hospitals in the surrounding communities of Georgetown and Paris. The group provides surgical consultation to several outlying clinics including those in Maysville, Paintsville, Fleming County, and Mt. Sterling. Providing the highest quality care to patients is what United Surgical Associates strives for each and every day. The success in doing so is evident by the thousands of people from all around Kentucky who seek treatment from United each year.

United Surgical Associates has high standards for each surgeon in its practice. Their philosophy is that if each surgeon buys into an established set of principles, the practice will achieve clinical and business excellence. Each surgeon must have integrity, be

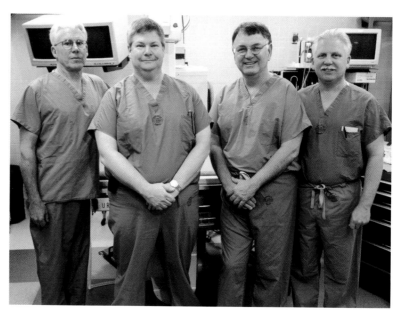

Michael Daugherty, MD; Colby Atkins, MD; Edwin Nighbert, MD; and Dennis Newton, MD; of Surgical Associates Division of United Surgical Associates. PHOTO BY STEWART BOWMAN

Lori Atkins, MD of Lexington Women's Diagnostic Center and Russ Shearer of Bluegrass Surgical Group, both divisions of United Surgical Associates. PHOTO BY STEWART BOWMAN

technically skilled, highly rated during training, and be proud of his or her work. Surgeons must have a humanistic outlook and demonstrate humility in approaching the uncertainties of medicine. They must be willing to learn the business side of surgical practices, yet see the value in living a healthy and comfortable home life. All physicians who are brought into the group should view their partnership as long-term and demonstrate loyalty to the group.

Each physician is certified by the American Board of Surgery. Subspecialty certification in vascular, oncology, and colorectal surgery are represented as well. There is an emphasis on continuing education to ensure physicians are kept up-to-date with the latest medical findings and surgical techniques.

Many of the practice's surgeons are native Kentuckians or received their education and training in Kentucky. These surgeons hold a special place in their hearts for the area and are committed to providing the best quality care for its residents.

By offering comprehensive surgical care, the group has maintained a large patient load. There are very few surgical procedures that the group's surgeons cannot provide. United's specialty, general surgery, covers vascular conditions such aneurysms, stroke, and vessel problems in the legs and feet; breast disease;

Oscar Mendiondo, MD leads the newest division, United Radiation Oncology. PHOTO BY STEWART BOWMAN

colonoscopy and gastroscopy are performed. United has a certified vascular laboratory for evaluation of peripheral circulatory disease. This enables United's physicians to detect problems in the arteries of the neck, the abdominal aorta, or lower extremity arterial and venous disease primarily through ultrasound technology. These studies may eliminate the need for in-hospital tests. The laboratory also helps physicians follow a patient's post surgical recovery. The practice owns a sclerolaser, a device that treats abnormal spider veins. Injection sclerotherapy in the office and minimally invasive outpatient surgery is available for treating varicose veins.

In the ever-changing work of healthcare, United Surgical Associates will strive to achieve two main objectives: to maintain a practice large enough to handle contractual obligations with the various healthcare delivery services, and to be a self-directed, self-controlled entity, able to administer the highest quality and most appropriate healthcare to Central Kentuckians. •

abdominal surgery; oncologic disease; colorectal problems; hernias, and laparoscopic procedures.

United Surgical Associates is committed to diagnosing and treating cancer. The Lexington Women's Diagnostic Center, operated by mammographic radiology specialists, is geared specifically toward diagnosing and treating breast cancer. Stereotactic breast biopsies are performed by both surgeons and radiologists. Bone density tests to evaluate osteoporosis are performed as well. In 2001, the practice opened United Radiation Oncology Associates. This center offers radiation therapy for many forms of cancer, including lung, breast, prostate, and colorectal.

United's close relationship with Lexington's major community hospitals allows convenience for patients requiring hospitalization. A patient needing to stay one or more nights in the hospital is scheduled to stay at the hospital most convenient to his or her family. United's physicians are patient advocates first while dealing with the full spectrum of contemporary insurance plans and regulations. If at-home care is needed, United's friendly staff helps patients locate a reputable source. For medical emergencies and "after hour" needs, one of United's physicians is always available 24 hours a day, seven days a week.

Modern technology is important to any medical practice. Office sigmoidoscopy and hospital

Edwin Rogers, MD and Peter Tate MD of Lexington Surgeons division of United Surgical Associates. PHOTO BY STEWART BOWMAN

BLUEGRASS ORTHOPAEDICS

As more and more people lead busy, fast-paced lifestyles, the affects of strenuous activity are catching up. Repetitive work creates joint problems. Contact sports can lead to injuries of the knee, shoulder, spine, and head. Car accidents can result in similar injuries that are even more traumatic in nature. With the increase of injuries and disease that afflict the musculoskeletal system, the need for treatment and care of such afflictions has increased.

Left to right: Dr.'s Norman Ellingsen, Howard Markowitz, Thomas Cervoni, Harry Lockstadt, John Balthrop, Frank Burke, Veronica Vasicek, and Greg D'Angelo. PHOTO BY STEWART BOWMAN

In 1988, Dr. Frank Burke, a board-certified orthopaedic surgeon, had a vision to create an "orthopaedic center of excellence." This vision became a reality when he founded Bluegrass Orthopaedics in Lexington. The practice's philosophy is to continually strive for clinical, service, and business excellence.

Now, Bluegrass Orthopaedics treats thousands of Central Kentuckians who suffer from a variety of musculoskeletal problems. At press time, Bluegrass Orthopaedics boasted eight surgeons, five physician assistants, and 44 support personnel. Dr. Frank Burke, Dr. Gregory D'Angelo, Dr. John Balthrop, Dr. Thomas Cervoni, and Dr. Veronica Vasicek specialize in general orthopaedics, sports medicine, arthroscopy, and total joint replacements. A unique treatment performed by Dr. Burke is Carticel implantation. This surgical procedure involves biopsy processing and cell culturing to help regenerate cartilage in an injured knee.

Bluegrass Orthopaedics has two spine surgeons: Dr. Harry Lockstadt who specializes in anterior and posterior back fusions, and Dr. Howard Markowitz whose specialty is lumbar and cervical spine. He performs outpatient vertebroplasty on patients with osteoporosis. This cutting-edge technology involves injecting a cement-like substance into

fractured vertebrae, providing lift, stability, and pain relief. Dr. Norman Ellingsen's focus is total shoulder, elbow, knee, and hip replacement and revision.

Accessibility to medical treatment is important to Bluegrass Orthopaedics' patients. Each physician is on staff with a local hospital, giving them access to state-of-the-art facilities across Lexington and Central Kentucky. For patients in surrounding counties, the practice runs clinics in nearby Lancaster, Harrodsburg, Georgetown, and Richmond. Physicians are on call 24 hours a day, seven days a week. The practice is full-service, providing everything from diagnosis, to surgery, to physical therapy services. The physicians and staff believe that the healing process depends on more than a single treatment but on a plan of treatments. Their approach is not about shortcuts or drive-through care. It's about optimizing around patients, serving them better and more effectively.

The practice recognizes that teamwork is key to providing the best in orthopaedic care to patients. Surgery is not always the answer to musculoskeletal ailments. When it is obvious that a patient will be better served by another type of treatment, the

Dr.'s Harry Lockstadt and Greg D'Angelo viewing a computerized patient chart. PHOTO BY STEWART BOWMAN

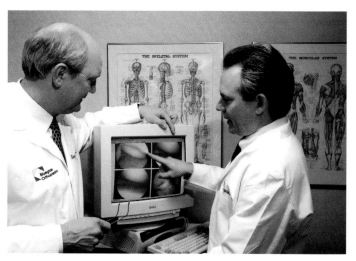

patient is referred to the practice's physical therapy department or to wherever the proper treatment can be administered.

Bluegrass Orthopaedics has placed special emphasis on educating patients about their injuries and disorders and how to help the healing process. A patient education coordinator invites patients and their families to review videos and pamphlets, and discuss upcoming surgery or therapy in a comfortable and relaxed atmosphere. Patients are encouraged to express issues or concerns they have prior to treatment to ensure they are comfortable with the procedure and relieve pre-treatment anxiety.

Osteoporosis is a debilitating bone disease that affects thousands of elderly people each year. It is the most common disease to affect the bones, yet many people are unfamiliar with it. As men and women age, they lose bone mass and become more susceptible to hip and wrist fractures, back pain, periodontal disease, and the loss of height. Women are particularly susceptible to the disease because of smaller, thinner bones and a loss of estrogen after menopause. Bluegrass Orthopaedics recognized the increasing need for treatment of this disease and began a special Osteoporosis program. Through this program, over 4,000 bone density scans are performed each year, allowing thousands of people to get the proper treatment to prevent or curb the crippling disease.

Open MRI (magnetic resonance imaging) is another modern diagnostic imaging technique that Bluegrass Orthopaedics has incorporated into their practice. Unlike CT scans, MRI works without radiation. The MRI tool uses magnetic fields and a sophisticated computer to take high-resolution pictures of bones and soft tissues. Patients do not feel any pain while undergoing

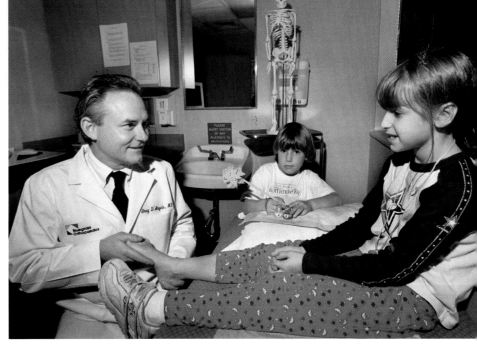

Doctor Greg D'Angelo with a patient. PHOTO BY STEWART BOWMAN

an MRI, but the machine may be noisy. An MRI helps the physician diagnose torn knee ligaments and cartilage, torn rotator cuffs, herniated disks, hip and pelvic problems, and other musculoskeletal conditions.

Physical Therapy is another area of concentration for Bluegrass Orthopaedics. Patients who are injured and in pain, but do not necessarily need surgery, are treated by the Physical Therapy department. Those recuperating from orthopaedic surgery, in large part, need some sort of physical therapy to properly heal. The practice's physical therapists work in conjunction with the physicians to provide total quality care to patients. This important team provides physical rehabilitation, work hardening, and testing to determine functional capacity, range of motion, and level of nerve and muscle function. The ultimate goal is to help patients understand their conditions, recover the use of affected joints and muscles, and return them to work and engage in everyday activity.

Bluegrass Orthopaedics stays current on state-of-the-art technology, drugs, and techniques in orthopaedic care. The practice runs BGMR, a research program that utilizes the latest in drug therapy and surgical instrumentation. Patients who participate in the program may qualify for medication and follow-up visits at no charge.

The physicians and staff of Bluegrass Orthopaedics know what it means to provide total quality care for patients. They understand the need for timely, efficient, and cost effective treatment for those suffering from orthopaedic ailments. As people lead more and more active lives, Bluegrass Orthopaedics will be prepared to respond to the ever-changing needs of the healthcare market and will work to remain a center of excellence in orthopaedic care. •

Bluegrass Medical Pavilion. PHOTO BY STEWART BOWMAN

CENTRAL KENTUCKY RADIOLOGY, PLLC

The 1950s were an exciting time for Lexington and the central Kentucky region. The city was growing at an unprecedented pace and more and more people were choosing to settle in the bustling town. With the surge of new residents came the need for bigger healthcare facilities and more physicians. At that time, two small physician groups operating in different hospitals in the central Kentucky area initiated their practices in diagnostic radiology.

Over the next several decades, Associates in Radiology and Dochterman, Caudill, and Riley became the standard of excellence in the field of diagnostic imaging in the greater Lexington area. Their respective practices grew in both stature and expanse of radiology services offered. The two groups served most physicians in the area and literally thousands of central Kentuckians over the years, offering the very latest in radiology technology with the highest quality service.

As the skyline of Lexington changed, so did the healthcare environment in the area. Despite the turbulence of the '90s that marked the end for several so-called healthcare giants, the two practices quietly continued to thrive and grow. The groups adapted by gaining new skills and improving efficiency in their service while remaining focused on quality. Referring physicians continued to place their confidence and their patient's diagnosis in the hands of these competent radiologists who were now becoming a tradition in central Kentucky healthcare.

In 1998, the two groups agreed to meet the next frontier as a single force. These practices were forged into Central Kentucky Radiology, one of the largest radiology practices in the state. This new entity, comprised of all board-certified physicians, offered a comprehensive array of diagnostic and interventional radiology services. Today, CKR serves hospitals, freestanding

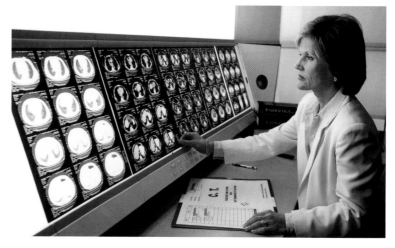

Dr. Christine Riley examines films for diagnostic radiology. PHOTO BY STEWART BOWMAN

imaging facilities, physician offices, and specialty medical facilities. Additionally, the company operates both MRI and mammography centers.

A lot has happened in Lexington over the past few decades. The population continues to expand—new neighborhoods spring up and thrive and new faces appear daily. Today, Lexington is a strong regional center for education, banking, retail, and healthcare. Yet, even with all of this growth, the traditions of Lexington remain, as always, distinct and proud. There is simply no other place like it.

So, too, are the miracles of modern medicine. Advances in healthcare and new medical technologies will continue to improve the quality of life for all Lexingtonians. And, you can be sure that a special group of dedicated radiologists will be leading the way, offering the latest in diagnostic and interventional radiology while maintaining focus on quality and service. Central Kentucky Radiology—a distinct and proud tradition that continues to grow along with the city it calls home, Lexington. •

Dr. Dale Absher performing interventional procedures. PHOTO BY STEWART BOWMAN

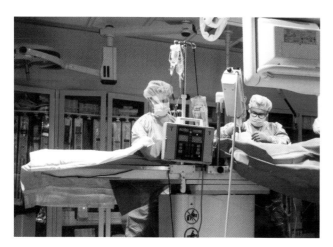

Education & Quality of Life, Hospitality & Tourism

UNIVERSITY OF KENTUCKY

To say that Lexington is a "college town" is an understatement. Lexington and the surrounding Bluegrass region is home to over a dozen colleges and universities. The most prominent higher education provider is the University of Kentucky, the state's flagship university and Kentucky's ninth largest economic enterprise.

Located near the heart of the city on a 685-acre campus, the University of Kentucky, or "UK" as most residents, students, and alumni call it, is one of a small sampling of universities with a teaching and research campus, a medical center, and a community college, all in one central location. It is the state's only public land-grant university dedicated to teaching, research, and service.

The almost 31,000 full- and part-time students who attend UK can choose from over 200 degree programs in 16 academic or professional colleges: Agriculture, Allied Health Professions,

The elation of graduation.

Researchers hold the key to unlocking the mysteries of Parkinson's and Alzheimer's disease.

Architecture, Arts and Sciences, Business and Economics, Communications and Information Studies, Dentistry, Education, Engineering, Fine Arts, Human Environmental Sciences, Law, Medicine, Nursing, Pharmacy, and Social Work.

Twenty-two varsity sports are available to student-athletes, the most visible being the UK men's basketball program, seven-time national champions of the coveted NCAA tournament. Over 250 campus organizations provide students an opportunity for a more well-rounded experience, ranging from educational, to social, to political groups.

UK's world-class faculty features some 1,800 full-time members and 98 percent hold the highest degree attainable in their field. Over 200 endowed chairs and professorships help to attract the best scholars and researchers that education has to offer.

UK is the region's largest employer, with some 10,500 employees. The university is directly linked to more than 78,000 other jobs in manufacturing, construction, technology, and service, many fueled by student, employee, and visitor spending.

Nobel, Pulitzer, Rhodes, Fulbright, Guggenheim, Grammy, Metropolitan Opera, and other prestigious panels have honored myriad UK students, faculty, and alumni.

UK has earned 42 national rankings—and counting—for quality education and research from such reputable agencies as

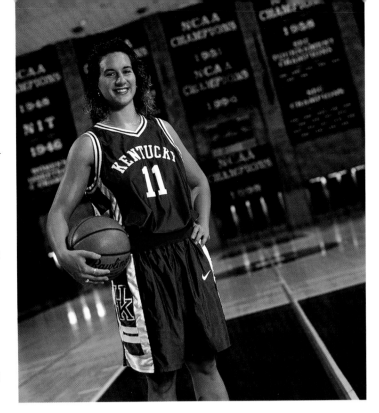

UK boasts 22 varsity sports.

the National Research Council and the National Institutes of Health. UK's book endowment, for example, is the largest among public universities and ranks second only to Harvard's.

Some of UK's other impressive academic and research rankings include:

- Four programs in the top five: Clinical Laboratory Science (1st), College of Pharmacy (3rd), Patterson School of Diplomacy (top 4), Martin School's Public Finance program (5th)
- 10th for academic supercomputers
- 15th among land-grant universities for patent and licensing income
- 32nd among public universities for research expenditures
- Top 100 colleges recommended for African Americans

According to *U.S. News & World Report*, UK's College of Law ties for third in the nation for job placement, just behind Harvard and Duke, placing an astounding 99 percent of all students in jobs. Similarly, 99 percent of College of Agriculture graduates find a job in their field within one year of graduation, as do 97 percent of social work graduates and 94 percent of UK's engineering graduates.

For those students who need additional help securing a job after graduation, UK boasts one of the largest career centers in the nation, with an on-site library, videoconferencing, and more than 15 interview rooms for corporate recruiting.

In the late 1990s, UK officials set an aggressive goal of becoming "America's next great university." The primary objective of this effort is to become one of the nation's top-20 public research universities. UK now measures its progress against a new set of benchmark institutions—the nation's elite—that raise the standard for academic and research achievement.

In light of this goal, Kentucky's Governor Paul Patton and the 1998 Kentucky General Assembly established the Research Challenge Trust Fund as an incentive to improve and enhance the state's higher education programs. Of $110 million in state support, UK was eligible for $66.7 million in matching funds. If UK privately raised that amount, the state would match it dollar-for-dollar. UK met the challenge in just one year and the program was renewed in 2000, enabling the university to nearly triple its number of endowed faculty positions available to recruit the world's best intellectual talent.

The Research Challenge Trust Fund became the first step in UK's comprehensive $600 million fund-raising campaign, the state's largest of its kind. In just two years, nearly two-thirds of the goal has been raised for academic and research support.

Another sign of UK's advances is an explosion of new construction on campus. In 2000, a new facility to house computer networking research, academic instruction, and outreach efforts was completed, while a new biomedical science research building, engineering complex, and allied health facility were under way. This caps a decade of expansion that included 41 new construction projects and 34 renovations.

Looking to the future, the University of Kentucky has a lot to do. With aggressive fund-raising efforts from private sources, support from the Kentucky legislature, and strong leadership to guide the process, UK's goal of becoming "America's next great university" is certainly within reach. •

Angelo Henderson, one of four Pulitzer Prize-winning UK graduates.

LEXINGTON THEOLOGICAL SEMINARY

Founded in 1865, Lexington Theological Seminary is deeply rooted in Central Kentucky as the oldest professional ministerial school related to the Christian Church (Disciples of Christ). Then known as The College of the Bible, the Seminary was originally one of several colleges in Kentucky University, the institution from which both Transylvania University and the University of Kentucky trace their roots. In 1878, the school became a separately chartered institution on Kentucky University's campus.

Bosworth Memorial Library. PHOTO BY STEWART BOWMAN

John W. McGarvey became the Seminary's most influential leader for several decades after the Civil War and is credited with stressing a detailed knowledge of the Bible at the center of the school's curriculum. But in 1912, sweeping changes in the Seminary's faculty brought new liberal ideas about the school's curriculum. These new faculty members lobbied for a broad theological liberalism and were met with much resistance from their conservative counterparts. Despite talk of a "heresy trial," the liberals gained control of the college in 1917.

In 1936, undergraduate degrees were required for admission to the College. Two years later, the College was listed as one of forty-six charter members of the Association of Theological Schools, the official accrediting agency for theological seminaries in the U.S. and Canada. By 1950, the College achieved complete

independence by relocating to pristine grounds across from the University of Kentucky campus. After celebrating its centennial in 1965, The College of the Bible officially changed its name to Lexington Theological Seminary to reflect a more contemporary image as a diverse, ecumenical, graduate theological seminary.

The Seminary continues to be a center of theological instruction in Central Kentucky. Its mission is to educate and train ministers for service in the Church and to serve the church as a theological resource and center of continuing education for ordained ministers and lay leaders. Although most of the students are affiliated with the Christian Church (Disciples of Christ), the school is ecumenical and caters to a long list of Christian denominations. Annual enrollment is approximately 200 and the student body exemplifies diversity stemming from geographic background, gender, undergraduate education, race, nationality, and ethnic origin.

In general, about 50 percent of students are women, and in the 1998-99 academic year, women exceeded men for the first time.

Although most students come from the immediate geographical area, the Seminary attracts students from all over the country and the world. This is, in part, due to the large number of churches located in the Central Kentucky area, which offer students a wide variety of opportunities to serve in the church. The high quality of life in Central Kentucky and close proximity to the University of Kentucky are also credited with attracting students from all over the globe. Participation in the Theological Education Association of Mid-America (TEAM-A), a consortium of five graduate theological schools affiliated with five different denominations, enhances the Seminary's diverse identity. This program offers students the opportunity

Meditation Garden. PHOTO BY STEWART BOWMAN

Campus entry plaza. PHOTO BY WALT JOHNSON

to study abroad and invites international scholars to be a part of the faculty. The Seminary upholds the belief that such diversification greatly enhances a student's leadership ability in the church.

Although the Seminary's primary focus is on preparation for pastoral ministry, its programs may also prepare students for specialized ministries such as Christian education, youth ministry, institutional chaplaincy and campus ministry. The Seminary's degree programs are accredited by the Commission on Colleges of the Southern Association of Colleges and Schools. Students may choose from several Masters programs geared toward enhancing their understanding of theological instruction and the Bible. A Master of Divinity degree is for persons who want to be ordained as ministers and requires a minimum three years of full-time study to complete. A Master of Arts degree is designed to prepare men and women for various forms of non-ordained ministry in the church, or for advanced graduate study in one of the theological disciplines. This degree is not for people who intend to be ordained. For Roman Catholic students, there are two Masters programs from which to choose: the

Master of Arts in Pastoral Studies and the Master of Arts in Religious Education. This M.A. program was borne out of a demand from Catholic lay people to expand their knowledge in scripture, spirituality or education and prepare for lay ministries in the church.

For ordained ministers, a Doctor of Ministry degree provides an opportunity to continue their education in the ministry. The program has three basic goals: to raise the standards of ordained ministry to an advanced level of integrating theology and the practice of ministry; to encourage and enable candidates to explore an ecclesial issue in their practice of ministry in the congregation or church agency they serve; and to express the Seminary's commitment to the continuing renewal and transformation of the church.

The Seminary is also a resource to the church. The Lay School of Theology offers lay people an opportunity to further their understanding of theology and the Bible with two-to three-week short courses.

The future is bright for Lexington Theological Seminary. Upgrades in technology have helped the school become current with new teaching and communications techniques. A new state-of-the-art library is slated for groundbreaking during the first decade in the new millennium. A new chapel is also planned to meet the changing worship styles of a new century. Staff members are continually exploring cooperative educational relationships with other denominations and hope to develop more formal, structured relationships with these churches. Lexington Theological Seminary will continue to improve its educational programs to fit the ever-changing needs of the church. •

Graduation day procession. PHOTO BY WALT JOHNSON

SULLIVAN UNIVERSITY

Five faculty members and seven students. That's who the father/son team of A.O. and A.R. Sullivan greeted the first day of classes in 1962 at Sullivan Business College, a one-year career school based in Louisville, Kentucky. The duo founded the college on the belief that they were creating a curriculum so much in demand, and at such a high quality, students would flock to the institution. And it proved to be so.

A tree lined campus green welcomes over 1,500 students year round. PHOTO BY STEWART BOWMAN

That same year during the fall semester, more than 150 students enrolled in Sullivan Business College. The growth this institution has experienced since then is nothing short of phenomenal, as it has become Kentucky's largest independent four-year college or university.

In 1972, Sullivan had grown to more than 700 students and began awarding associate degrees. The next year, the college merged with Bryant and Stratton Business College in Louisville, adding a century-long tradition to Sullivan's resume. And, in 1979, Sullivan became the first privately owned collegiate institution in the South to receive Collegiate Accreditation from the prestigious Commission on Colleges of the Southern Association of Colleges and Schools. Students could now receive two-year degrees from the school.

It was in 1985 that Sullivan opened a branch campus in Lexington and, in 1990, the college added bachelor's degrees and received regional accreditation as a four-year college.

In 1997, Sullivan College took the next step toward higher learning with the establishment

The Learning Resource Center provides state-of-the art technology and a stimulating atmosphere. PHOTO BY STEWART BOWMAN

of a Graduate School of Business and the addition of a Master in Business Administration (MBA) degree. This newfound status prompted a name change in 2000 to "Sullivan University." In 2000, the university added a new Master of Science in Managing Information Technology degree and is planning to add a Master of Science in Hospitality Management.

Now, Sullivan University's Lexington campus resides on a 10-acre site that serves more than 1,500 students a year. The main campus in Louisville also has grown to over 2,500 students and a nearby Fort Knox, Kentucky extension campus serves both civilian and military personnel.

Sullivan University still holds the title as Kentucky's largest private four-year college or university, with more than 4,000 students enrolled at presstime. Key to the university's growth on its three Kentucky campuses is its career-first upside-down curriculum that allows students to decide how far they want to go, for how long. Students may choose to enroll for a one-year diploma, a two-year associate degree followed by full-time employment, or continue study for a four-year bachelor's degree, or even a master's degree.

Maintaining enrollment in a career college can be challenging but Sullivan University has an innovative incentive that keeps students coming back. The university gives a guarantee that once a student enrolls in a program and remains in continuous enrollment, tuition will not increase through the completion of a bachelor's degree. Students are able to budget for tuition costs each year without the worry of hard-hitting tuition increases.

Also key to student retention is that the university offers year-round classes. For students anxious to begin their careers, they can choose to attend year-round, potentially finishing a diploma program in nine months or an associate degree in as few as 18 months. And this

Landscaped areas provide great places to study and socialize. PHOTO BY STEWART BOWMAN

isn't just convenient for students. Employers also need new employees throughout the year and have come to depend on Sullivan to provide a pool of students to fill these positions. Sullivan also offers classes on the weekend, at night, and on-line. Although year-round operation helps students receive education and training in a timely fashion, Sullivan does understand the importance of free time. Operating on a four-day academic week, "Plus Friday" is utilized for accelerated or tutorial time with faculty.

Recognizing the large employment base driven by the hospitality and culinary industries, Sullivan University created a National Center for Hospitality Studies in 1987 on the Louisville campus. The hospitality industry offers numerous worldwide career options in administration and management for graduates interested in careers with restaurants, private clubs, hospitals, travel agencies, hotels and motels, educational institutions, catering, airlines, convention planning, cruise lines, and the food brokerage business. The National Center for Hospitality Studies prepares students for careers in the hospitality field by offering five Associate of Science (A.S.) Degree majors and a bachelor's degree in Hospitality Management.

In light of its move to university status, Sullivan established the "Global Online" study program in 2000. The new program expanded the university's on-line capabilities to offer both undergraduate and graduate level programs worldwide.

One of the major differences between Sullivan University and other two- and four-year colleges and universities is its commitment to assisting graduates with career development in their field of study.

The success of this effort is best illustrated by the university's graduate employment record which achieved 99.2 percent success in 2000. In fact, this percentage has not been lower than 97.8 percent since 1988. A graduate employment staff works year-round matching graduates to positions locally, nationally, and worldwide.

Unique to Sullivan University is their "lifetime review privilege" which allows any graduate to return and take any course previously studied at no charge. And the privilege of being a Sullivan alum does not end there. The university has fee-free lifetime employment assistance available to graduates—once, twice, or as many times as they like throughout their working career.

Sullivan's unmatched success at placing graduates and alumni in jobs is, in large part, due to their continuous effort to develop relationships and stay informed on employers' wants and needs. The university provides custom-tailored pre-screening of job applicants, offers on-campus interview facilities, hosts a Career Expo and job fairs, and maintains a number of industry advisory boards.

As Sullivan University continues to grow, the faculty and administration are dedicated to adhering to one basic principle: students come first. With a third generation of Sullivan family leadership, Sullivan University looks forward to keeping this high standard of education while meeting the challenges of the 21st century. •

Personal and approachable faculty make learning a positive experience. PHOTO BY STEWART BOWMAN

LEXINGTON COMMUNITY COLLEGE

*I*t was in 1965 that Lexington Community College, or LCC as most locals call it, opened its doors to students seeking a brighter future for themselves. Its mission was to grant associate degrees to a diverse body of students eager to build solid foundations for university transfer, satisfying employment, and lifelong learning, all at an affordable cost. Located on the University of Kentucky campus, the state's flagship university, LCC was then part of UK's 14-member community college system.

LCC's vision is to become one of the top 20 community colleges in the United States. PHOTO BY DAVID COYLE

In 1997, The Postsecondary Education Improvement Act realigned 13 of the community colleges with the state's technical schools. LCC remained a part of the University of Kentucky.

Now LCC is the only community college affiliated with the University of Kentucky. Under the umbrella of UK, LCC has a unique partnership with the university. Very few universities throughout the nation boast such a strong relationship to a community college and the benefit to LCC and UK is significant.

LCC students have access to UK's infinite educational resources and extracurricular activities. The college itself is involved in UK's strategic planning process and is included in priorities and goals for the university. The administrations of both schools have set an aggressive goal for LCC to become a national model for community colleges.

UK benefits from the LCC partnership with a large number of student transfers from LCC to UK. Not only do these students provide larger enrollment numbers, they are better prepared to successfully complete a four-year degree program.

For students planning to transfer to UK or another four-year institution, LCC offers two degrees: Associate in Arts and an Associate in Science. A two-year Associate in Applied Science degree is valuable for students planning to join the workforce upon graduation, due to an increase in the demand for employees

with technical skills. LCC offers an Associate in Applied Science degree in 14 technical areas: Architectural Technology; Business Technology; Civil Engineering Technology; Computer Information Systems; Dental Hygiene; Dental Laboratory Technology; Early Childhood Education; Engineering Technology; Environmental Science Technology; Nuclear Medicine Technology; Nursing; Office Systems; Radiography; and Respiratory Care

And for those students already in the workforce needing to grow their current set of skills, LCC has the Continuing Education & Workforce Development Center. The center assists businesses throughout the state by fulfilling "just-in-time" training needs for employees and providing a variety of professional certification programs.

Looking to the future, LCC will continue its commitment to providing open access to quality education for its growing and diverse community. As technology continues to advance, LCC will strive to remain a leader in educating and training a workforce capable of meeting business and industry needs. And in partnership with the University of Kentucky, the college will enhance and improve programs in order to become the model for community colleges throughout the nation. •

President Kerley, center, chats with LCC Student Ambassadors (left to right) Jeffrey Mosher, Erin Young, Sara Evans, and Monica Scott. PHOTO BY DAVID COYLE

BLUE GRASS TOURS

Visitors from all over the world have traveled far and near to behold the rolling hills of Lexington's breathtaking bluegrass countryside. White fences line miles of green pastures where majestic Thoroughbreds graze, gallop, and play. Since its inception in 1961, Blue Grass tours has sought to share the sights and sounds of the Bluegrass with the throngs of people who visit the area each year.

In 1978, a young Lexingtonian named Wallace Jones, Jr. saw the potential of Blue Grass Tours and purchased the company from its original owner. He immediately began running more tours with a new fleet of vans. But the most significant move Jones made within the first few years of owning Blue Grass Tours was leasing a bus for large tours. This generated so much business for the company that it wasn't long before Jones was situated to purchase a bus for Blue Grass Tours.

About a year later, the tour company bought a second bus, and this time it would be brand new. Like a proud father, Jones showed off his new prize possession by putting it on display on the corner of Main and Vine streets in downtown Lexington. He gave the bus a shiny new paint job, in blue and white, the colors of the city's home team, the University of Kentucky Wildcats. Across the side of the bus was the company name and phone number. Blue Grass Tours' phone starting ringing off the hook.

Now, Blue Grass Tours serves groups across Kentucky, the United States, and Canada. The company provides local horse farm and attraction tours to convention delegates in Lexington and other nearby cities. It serves school groups who visit such exciting venues as Washington D.C., Orlando, Florida, and Chicago, Illinois. Colleges and universities of all sizes utilize the company's transportation services.

Blue Grass Tours resides in a 12,000-square-foot facility on a 3.5-acre lot in Lexington's industrial area. Some 50 people work for the company in tour guide, motorcoach operator, mechanic, maintenance, and administrative positions. The company owns up to 19 vehicles, including 47- and 56- passenger motorcoaches, a 26-passenger minicoach, a 20-passenger custom motorcoach, and a 120-inch stretch limousine, along with three 15-passenger vans.

55-passenger motorcoach and 14-passenger tour van. PHOTO BY DAVID COYLE

Blue Grass Tours attributes its success to remaining current on market trends, diversifying services when appropriate, and following the law in such a heavily regulated business. Its stellar reputation as a safety-conscious tour operator has also been key to the success of the business. With a hard-working, dedicated staff, a keen sense of the market, and a cutting-edge approach to new technology, Blue Grass Tours will remain a competitive provider of tours for groups all over Kentucky and the nation. •

Eight-passenger stretch Lincoln limousine. PHOTO BY DAVID COYLE

KENNEDY BOOK STORE

After serving his country during World War II, Joe Kennedy returned home to attend college at Indiana University. While a student, he began working for the university's bookstore and quickly realized the great business potential of the used book market. It wasn't long before he began looking for a bookstore location of his own. And he didn't have to look far. Lexington, Kentucky was just a short jaunt from home and boasted the state's signature university, the University of Kentucky.

Kennedy Book Store is surrounded by the University of Kentucky's beautiful campus.

Lexington's big state college/small quaint town combination was just right for Kennedy and his wife, Peggy, and in May of 1950, they opened Kennedy Book Store across the street from the university's main campus.

Early on, Kennedy held firm to the idea that if he kept a large inventory of used books in demand by students and the university, his business would succeed. He learned to think like a student—what he would want and need from a bookstore if he were back in school. His instincts proved accurate. Kennedy Book Store has since grown to become the number one supplier of textbooks to UK students. The bookstore's slogan "more used books" has been a cornerstone to its success.

Of course, a business cannot be successful without the hard work and dedication of its employees. The first Kennedy Book Store employee began in early 1950, eventually became general manager and remained with the bookstore until his retirement in 1991. The bookstore has always employed Kennedy family members and others who have upheld the same tradition Joe Kennedy started over a half-century ago. University of Kentucky students have always been a large part of Kennedy's employee roster, bringing an empathetic viewpoint to the business.

Another key factor for Kennedy Book Store's success has been diversifying its product line at appropriate times. As UK sports, particularly men's basketball, became more and more popular, the bookstore recognized a tremendous demand for sports memorabilia. A "rah-rah" section was added in response to this demand, offering UK sports merchandise to the spirited student body and supportive college town. A large section of the store is dedicated to art supplies, meeting the demand from students in creative and graphic arts programs and other fields of study.

With the introduction of the Internet and E-commerce in the late 1990s, Kennedy Book Store instantly became a worldwide business. It was one of the first businesses in Lexington to have a bona fide E-commerce website and has embraced this new technology ever since. Although textbooks are sold over the Internet, UK memorabilia is mostly requested by online consumers.

Kennedy Book Store is likely to always be a family-owned and operated business. But no matter who is at the helm, the bookstore intends to stay acutely aware of students needs, wants, and demands and continue its commitment to providing "more used books" to the university it loves so much, the University of Kentucky. •

Kennedy's Book Store is surrounded by the University of Kentucky's beautiful campus. PHOTO BY DAVID COYLE

THE COUNCIL OF STATE GOVERNMENTS

In 1933, states across the country were evolving their role in the federal system. Henry Toll, a statesman from Colorado, began a movement for state governments to share information on the best state practices and to have more influence on issues typically dictated by the federal government. That year, Toll founded the Council of State Governments, serving governors, legislators, constitutional elected officials, select agency heads, and justice officials.

Now headquartered on the outskirts of Lexington's lush Bluegrass countryside, The Council of State Governments, or CSG as it is called, acts as a central nervous system to all 50 U.S. states and five U.S. territories. It is a multi-branch organization that champions excellence in state government, working with state leaders across the nation to generate the best ideas and solutions for efficient and innovative state government operation. More specifically, CSG builds leadership skills to improve decision-making; advocates multi-state problem solving and partnerships; interprets changing national and international conditions; and promotes sovereignty of the states and their role in the American federal system.

CSG's Lexington headquarters serve as the central administrative agency, providing finance, human resources, and information systems services to all other CSG offices. The in-house production, publishing, marketing, and sales divisions are run by this office, as well as a dynamic policy research and public affairs shop, the States Information Center and seven of CSG's affiliated organizations.

Although its headquarters is in Lexington, CSG is regional in nature, with offices located strategically throughout the country. It is divided into four separate regions: Midwestern, Western, Eastern, and Southern. To ensure that its legislative and governor members can keep the pulse of what is happening on the federal

Dan Sprague is CSG's Executive Director. PHOTO BY STEWART BOWMAN

CSG's Headquarters office (shown above) is near the Kentucky Horse Park. PHOTO BY DAVID COYLE

level, a CSG office is also operated out of Washington, DC.

A primary function of CSG is to allow states to share ideas and successes with one another. There are a number of programs and services administered by CSG that put leaders together and promote useful dialogue. The Innovation Awards give states recognition for effective and innovative state programs, which are shared with the rest of the membership for replication. A leadership development program, the Henry Toll Fellowship program, helps state officials, judges and staff to become more effective and persuasive leaders. CSG's Annual Meeting and State Leadership Forum encourage dialogue between states, where ideas are exchanged and solutions to state issues are borne. An international program assists states in international trade, economic development and other global activities. And, keeping true to the mission of its founder, CSG promotes the sovereign interest of states at the federal level. The Council rewards members of Congress who advocate strong state roles with an annual award.

As political and social issues become more and more complex, The Council of State Governments stands ready to identify these trends, to generate creative ideas for change and to help states implement solutions. The ultimate goal: more efficient, effective state governments. •

BIBLIOGRAPHY

Promotional Literature

"Around the Town: Lexington and the Bluegrass." Published by Around the Town Communications, Inc., Lexington, Ky., July 1999.

"Historic Harrisburg: Kentucky's First Settlement." Published by Harrodsburg Mercer County Tourist Commission, Harrodsburg, Ky.

"Historic Shaker Village of Pleasant Hill." Distributed by Shaker Village of Pleasant Hill, Harrodsburg, Ky. Creative work by By Design. Printed by Gateway Press, Inc.

"Kentucky: Great Getaway Guide 2001." Published by the Kentucky Department of Travel, Frankfort, Ky., 2001.

"The Lexington Walk & Bluegrass Country Driving Tour." Published by the Lexington Convention and Visitors Bureau, Lexington, Ky.

"Visitors Planning Guide." Published by the Lexington Convention and Visitors Bureau, Lexington, Ky.

Web sites

American Hockey League: www.theahl.com

The Blood-Horse: www.bloodhorse.com

Blue Grass Airport: www.bluegrassairport.com

Calumet Farm: www.calumetfarm.com

Central Baptist Hospital: www.centralbap.com

Commonwealth of Kentucky: www.kydirect.net

The Festival of the Bluegrass: www.kyfestival.com

Greater Lexington Chamber of Commerce: www.lexchamber.com

Horse Mania: www.horsemania.org

Insiders' Guide—Lexington: www.insiders.com/lexington-ky

International Museum of the Horse: www.imh.org

Keeneland: www.keenland.com

The Kentucky Department of Travel: kentuckytourism.com

Kentucky Historical Society: www.state.ky.us/agencies/khs

Kentucky Horse Park: www.imh.org

Kentucky Thoroughblades: www.thoroughblades.com

Lexington Center Corporation: www.lexingtoncenter.com

Lexington Children's Museum: www.lfucg.com/childrensmuseum

Lexington Children's Theatre: www.lctonstage.org

Lexington Community College: www.uky.edu/LCC

Lexington Convention and Visitors Bureau: www.visitlex.com

Lexington Discovery: www.lexingtondiscovery.com

Lexington-Fayette Urban County Div. of Police: www.lexingtonpolice.lfucg.com

Lexington-Fayette Urban County Government: www.lfucg.com

Lexington Herald-Leader: www.kentuckyconnect.com/heraldleader

Lexington Legends: www.lexingtonlegends.com

Lexington Livery Carriage Company, Inc.: lexingtonlivery.com

Lexington Philharmonic: www.lexingtonphilharmonic.org

Maxwell H. Gluck Equine Research Center: www.uky.edu/Agriculture/VetScience/max.htm

Red Mile: www.tattersallsredmile.com

Samaritan Hospital: www.samaritanhospital.com

Shaker Village of Pleasant Hill: www.shakervillageky.org

The Thoroughbred Center: www.khc.org

Transylvania University: www.transy.edu/indexsm.shtml

University of Kentucky: www.uky.edu

University of Kentucky Athletics: www.ukathletics.com

University of Kentucky-Department of Horticulture: www.uky.edu/Agriculture/HLA/visitor.htm

ENTERPRISE INDEX

Ball Homes/Donamire Farm
PO Box 12950
Lexington, Kentucky 40583
Ball Homes:
Phone: 859-268-1191
Fax: 859-268-9093
Donamire Farm:
Phone: 859-233-3824
Fax: 859-255-8020
www.ballhomes.com
Pages 102-105

Baumann Paper Co.
1601 Baumann Road
Lexington, Kentucky 40511
Phone: 859-252-8891
        800-860-8891
Fax: 859-254-0579
E-mail: fbaumann@mis.net
www.baumannpaper.com
Page 98

Blue Grass Tours
817 Enterprise Drive
Lexington, Kentucky 40510
Phone: 859-233-2152
Fax: 859-255-4748
E-mail: bgt@lex.infi.net
www.bluegrasstours.com
Page 151

Bluegrass Orthopaedics
3480 Yorkshire Medical Park
Lexington, Kentucky 40509
Phone: 859-263-5140
Fax: 859-263-5141
www.bluegrassortho.com
Pages 138-139

Central Kentucky Radiology, PLLC
2365 Harrodsburg Road, Suite B-125
Lexington, Kentucky 40504
Phone: 859-219-9583
Fax: 859-219-9433
E-mail: jimfreedman@mindspring.com
Page 140

Cobra Farm
3030 Newtown Pike
Lexington, Kentucky 40511
Phone: 859-255-7966
Fax: 859-231-1122
www.cobrafarm.com
Pages 130-131

The Council of State Governments
2760 Research Park Drive
Lexington, Kentucky 40511
Phone: 859-244-8000
Fax: 859-244-8001
E-mail: info@csg.org
www.csg.org
Page 153

Cutter Homes
3131 Custer Drive
Lexington, Kentucky 40517
Phone: 859-273-2006
Fax: 859-271-4109
E-mail: cutter1@infi.net
www.cutterhomesltd.com
Pages 114-115

Don Jacobs
2689 Nicholasville Road
Lexington, Kentucky 40503
Phone: 859-276-3546
Fax: 859-278-0723
E-mail: djoadvertising@mindspring.com
www.donjacobs.com
Pages 106-107

**General Rubber and Plastics
  Company, Inc.**
1016 Majaun Road
Lexington, Kentucky 40511
Phone: 859-254-6436
Fax: 859-253-1922
E-mail: info@generalrubberplastics.com
www.generalrubberplastics.com
Page 96

**Greater Lexington Chamber of
  Commerce**
330 East Main Street, Suite 100
Lexington, Kentucky 40507
Phone: 859-254-4447
Fax: 859-233-3304
E-mail: info@lexchamber.com
www.lexchamber.com
Pages 112-113

Henkel-Denmark
1116 Manchester Street
Lexington, Kentucky 40508
Phone: 859-455-9577
Fax: 859-455-9126
E-mail:
  gordon.denmark@henkeldenmark.com
www.henkeldenmark.com
Page 118

**Holman Plumbing, Heating & Air
  Conditioning**
948 National Avenue
Lexington, Kentucky 40502
Phone: 859-255-6027
Fax: 859-231-0506
Page 119

Kennedy Book Store
405 South Limestone Street
Lexington, Kentucky 40508
Phone: 859-252-0331
        888-8GO-CATS
Fax: 859-254-0684
E-mail: kbs@kennedys.com
www.kennedys.com
Page 152

Kentucky Ear, Nose & Throat
1720 Nicholasville Road, Suite 501
Lexington, Kentucky 40503
Phone: 859-278-1114
Fax: 859-277-3425
E-mail: kyent@msn.com
www.myhealth.com/kentuckyearnosethroat
Pages 134-135

Lexington Community College
209 Oswald Building
Cooper Drive
Lexington, Kentucky 40506-0235
Phone: 859-257-4872
        866-774-4872
Fax: 859-257-5706
E-mail: lccinfo@lsv.uky.edu
www.uky.edu/lcc
Page 150

Lexington Herald-Leader
100 Midland Avenue
Lexington, Kentucky 40508-1999
Phone: 859-231-3100
www.kentucky.com
Page 120

Lexington Theological Seminary
631 South Limestone Street
Lexington, Kentucky 40508
Phone: 859-252-0361
Fax: 859-258-9167
E-mail: swray@lextheo.edu
www.lextheo.edu
Pages 146-147

The Mason & Hanger Group
  a Day & Zimmermann company
300 West Vine Street, Suite 1300
Lexington, Kentucky 40507-1814
Phone: 859-252-9980
Fax: 859-389-8870
E-mail: info@mhgrp.com
www.mhgrp.com
Page 117

Mill Ridge Farm
3414 Bowman Mill Road
Lexington, Kentucky 40513
Phone: 859-231-0606
Fax: 859-255-6010
E-mail: millridge@millridge.com
www.millridge.com
Pages 124-127

Oak Grove at Lexington
3901 Rapid Run Drive
Lexington, Kentucky 40515
Phone: 859-245-4481
        877-245-4481
Fax: 859-245-4747
E-mail: oakgrove@swhprop.com
www.swhprop.com
Pages 108-111

Rood & Riddle Equine Hospital
PO Box 12070
Lexington, Kentucky 40580
Phone: 859-233-0371
Fax: 859-255-5367
E-mail: rreh@roodandriddle.com
www.roodandriddle.com
Pages 128-129

Sullivan University
2355 Harrodsburg Road
Lexington, Kentucky 40504
Phone: 859-276-4357
Fax: 859-276-1153
www.sullivan.edu
Pages 148-149

The Trane Company
1515 Mercer Road
Lexington, Kentucky 40511
Phone: 859-259-2500
Fax: 859-259-2595
www.trane.com
Page 99

United Surgical Associates
1401 Harrodsburg Road, Suite B355
Lexington, Kentucky 40504
Phone: 859-277-5934
Fax: 589-277-5936
E-mail: surgunited@aol.com
http://unitedsurgical.md
Pages 130-137

University of Kentucky
Lexington, Kentucky 40506
Phone: 859-257-9000
Fax: 859-257-2635
www.uky.edu
Pages 144-145

The Valvoline Company
3499 Blazer Parkway
Lexington, Kentucky 40509
Phone: 859-357-7000
Fax: 859-357-2686
E-mail: makish@ashland.com
www.valvoline.com
Page 97

WKYT-TV
2851 Winchester Road
Lexington, Kentucky 40509
Phone: 859-299-0411
Fax: 859-299-5531
E-mail: wmartin@wkyt.com
www.wkyt.com
Page 116

INDEX

BIOGRAPHIES

DR. THOMAS D. CLARK
Author, Special Introduction

Dr. Thomas Clark retired as a distinguished professor of American History from the University of Kentucky in 1968 with an extensive knowledge of the state and its history. Born in Mississippi in 1903, Dr. Clark earned a degree from the University of Mississippi in 1929. He then went on to receive a master's degree from UK and a Ph.D. from Duke University. Having taught at UK for more than 30 years, Dr. Clark continued to serve as a professor to numerous colleges and universities for many years. Over his lifetime, Dr. Clark has received awards ranging from The Governor's Medal to the Distinguished Rural Kentuckian Award to an Award of Merit for State and Local History, and he has authored and edited more than a dozen history books and publications. Married with two children, three grandchildren, and three great-grandchildren, Dr. Clark resides in Lexington.

PAM MITCHELL MANGAS
Profile Writer

Pam Mitchell Mangas is president of Mitchell Marketing Communications, a full-service marketing, advertising, and public relations agency operating in Lexington, Kentucky. For nearly eight years, Pam served on the non-profit and corporate side of the communications industry in positions with Lexmark International, the Greater Lexington Chamber of Commerce, and the Lexington Convention and Visitors Bureau. After working as an account executive for a successful Lexington advertising agency, Pam recognized that her true niche was serving in this type of environment. Her agency, Mitchell Marketing Communications, is dedicated to helping organizations establish and maintain strategic marketing, advertising, and public relations campaigns that are successful year after year. She has volunteered for and offered her professional expertise to such worthy non-profit organizations as the Children's Miracle Network, Opportunity for Work and Learning, Inc., American Heart Association, and March of Dimes. Pam also is an active member of the Public Relations Society of America.

JEFF ROGERS
Featured Photographer

Jeff Rogers grew up in Corinth, Kentucky (population 250). Since completing a B.A. in Art, 1981 at Transylvania University, he has lived in Lexington. He has been a full time photographer and business owner since 1988. He has won numerous Addy awards and other honors such as receiving a Photo District News/Nikon self-promo award. His studio is located in historic Victorian Square in downtown Lexington. He exhibits on a frequent basis and his photography is regularly seen in publications that go around the globe. Memberships include a variety of professional and photography oriented organizations as well as being a lay speaker for the United Methodist Church. More of his work can be seen on his web site at www.jeffrogers.com.

PAT MCDONOGH
Featured Photographer

Pat McDonogh is a 1977 graduate of the University of Louisville with a major in Fine Arts. He has worked as a photographer for 22 years, the last 18 with the *Louisville Courier-Journal*. He has won numerous awards for his work, including sharing in the Pulitzer Prize for General Reporting.

His work has appeared in *Time, Newsweek, Sports Illustrated, Rolling Stone, Smithsonian,* and *Historic Preservation* magazines.

McDonogh's work was recently featured in the Japanese publication *I Magazine*. Two books of his work have been published, *Hoosiers* and *Louisville and its Environs*. He is married to the former Jeri Johnson and has two beautiful daughters from China, Lily, 5, and Rose, 1.

STEWART BOWMAN
Corporate Profile Photographer

Stewart Bowman, a native of Lexington, has covered central and eastern Kentucky for the *Louisville Courier-Journal* for over 22 years. He has won many regional and national awards for his work in Kentucky as well as Central America, including coverage of the aftermath of Hurricane Mitch in 1998.

DAVID COYLE
Corporate Profile Photographer

Lexington native David Coyle has been a freelance photographer since 1985. He is currently Director of Photography for the University of Kentucky Athletics Association.